JOHN BURTON-RACE

THE MAN, THE MAGIC
AND THE MAYHEM

JOHN BURTON-RACE

THE AUTHORISED BIOGRAPHY

with Michael Cowton

THE MAN, THE MAGIC & THE MAYHEM

Published in Great Britain in 2020
by Banovallum Books
an imprint of Mortons Books Ltd.
Media Centre
Morton Way
Horncastle LN9 6JR
www.mortonsbooks.co.uk

ISBN 978 1 911658 41 2

Typeset by Kelvin Clements
Printed and bound by Gutenberg Press, Malta

For my family, and in particular my grandchildren Luke, Ollie and Connie, beacons of light in an often-dark world.

*'Catch on fire with enthusiasm, and people will
come for miles to watch you burn.'*

JO ANN BUTLER

CONTENTS

INTRODUCTION

DEEP IN the Parahyangan Highlands, overlooking the northern reaches of Bandung, lays Mount Tangkuban Perahu. Its scenic beauty and closeness to the provincial capital of West Java, Indonesia, makes the broad, shield-like stratovolcano a magnet for tourists who daily hike to its volcanic rim. As they peer into the Domas Crater, sulphur fumes from the chamber rise to greet them. Frequent eruptions over a period of two hundred years caused colossal boulders to be carried down its flanks by lava flows, creating cliffs over which waterfalls plunged to form the vast lake which today covers the Bandung plain. It is perhaps understandable that, in these magnificent Parahyangan (Land of God) Highlands, myths and legends permeate from Tangkuban Perahu's distinctive, smouldering shape, often likened to an upturned boat; such is the translation from the ethnic Sundanese language.

One such legend tells of Sangkuriang, who had been separated from his mother since childhood. It was only thanks to the Gods that fate brought them together once again, after Sangkuriang stopped by a small village and had a chance encounter with a beautiful maiden, whom he fell in love with. The maiden, Dayang Sumbi, was, in fact, his mother, and had remained youthful throughout the years of their separation. It was not long before the realisation dawned on her of the true identity of her lover. Knowing they would never be together, she agreed to marry him only if he could complete the seemingly impossible task of building a dam and a boat in a single night. With the help of the spirit world, Sangkuriang set about his task. Realising he was about to complete it, Dayang Sumbi called on the Gods to cause the sun to rise before dawn was due, and with a wave of her magic shawl she lit up the Eastern horizon. The deception worked. Cocks crowed and farmers rose for another day of toil in the fields. With all his hard work undone, an enraged Sangkuriang kicked the boat, turning it upside down, thereby giving birth to the volcano's appearance and its unique name.

The legend was not lost on a young John Burton-Race, who would often gaze up at that same volcano from his home in Bandung. Indeed, Tangkuban Perahu could well be a metaphor for his life, such are the hyperboles and legendary outpourings so associated with his character. 'Sometimes I think I am on a boat that is upturned, and I am in the sea drowning. Every time I manage to scramble back on, I am flung off again.'

1

REALITY BITES

EARLY SUMMER in the quintessentially British seaside town of Torquay. Recognised for its superb beaches, it is easy to see why this stretch of Devon coastline is nicknamed the English Riviera. I am waiting for John Burton-Race in the lounge of the appropriately named John Burton-Race Hotel and Restaurant. I am early, deliberately so—this is the first occasion I am meeting the television celebrity and former double Michelin-starred chef. Having scanned dozens of Press clippings and re-watched the television series French Leave and Return Of The Chef on YouTube, I am slightly apprehensive, not really knowing what to expect, for Mr Burton-Race has excelled at both tradition and rebellion throughout his long and distinguished career. Never lost for words, his reputation—if you are wont to believe what you have read in the newspapers over the years—has been built around a fiery temperament, unpredictability and outspokenness.

As I shuffle through my paperwork, I am told that John has put a call through to reception. Apparently, I am in the right town but at the wrong hotel. John is waiting for me a ten-minute walk away along the promenade at the Grand Hotel. Not a great start on my account, as John had previously told me that if I were travelling by train, I would find the hotel adjacent to the railway station. If I were travelling by car, that would be a different matter entirely. And that is exactly what I had done. I abandon my vehicle at John Burton-Race Hotel and Restaurant and enjoy a pleasant walk along the sweeping promenade surprisingly devoid of people, considering the time of year.

In the fall of 2016, John, a long-time resident of Devon, formed a business partnership with Keith Richardson, owner of The Richardson Hotel Group, and embarked on a new challenge at the Grosvenor Hotel in Torquay. The company had purchased the property for £700,000 in 2012 from its previous owner, Mark Jenkins, who featured in the Channel 4 reality show The Hotel, showcasing the backroom antics of the wacky owner and his exasperated staff. The aim was to offer guests a combination of luxury accommodation and award-winning fine dining. There was, however, a major stumbling block to overcome first. Despite being one of the main hotels on Belgrave Road, the rundown Victorian pile was in serious need of renovation in order to return the building to its former glory, with upgraded rooms and facilities befitting the guests. Set in an excellent location and surrounded by beautiful gardens a mere stone's throw from the seafront, it is easy to imagine the attraction for John, who threw himself into the challenge, taking charge of the kitchen re-design, menu planning and food preparation. Fast forward to 2018. With the transformation complete, so began a new chapter for the hotel with a re-brand to the John Burton-Race Restaurant With Rooms. The original concept was for the property to seep into the public consciousness as a modern and stylish French-type Auberge and be named accordingly. Check in, dine and relax; a philosophy that has been steadily gaining ground across the country, whereby diners take full advantage of a gourmet dining experience and sample an expertly chosen wine list, with the added benefit of an overnight stay. However, the marketing gurus within the company then went into reverse mode, considering the fashionable branding a stretch too far when there were multiple bedrooms to fill on a regular basis, so they promptly re-named it the John Burton-Race Hotel and Restaurant. Whatever the benefits of hindsight, Torquay diners suddenly found themselves treated to a unique blend of traditional service excellence and modern creative cuisine thanks to John's formidable culinary influences of innovation, and the best of British produce visible in his seasonally focused menu.

For John, the vision was to raise awareness within Devon and further afield that lovers of great food do not need to pay astronomical prices to enjoy a gourmet dining experience, and he believed he had landed on the perfect platform upon which to showcase his passion for food and locally sourced produce. Attracted by the county's own microclimate, it is Devon where he feels most at home, surrounded by a natural larder of all-year-round tender lamb, scallops from Babbacombe, crabs from Dartmouth and oysters from Bigbury. It was a recipe for success, with the restaurant soon the recipient of two AA Rosettes.

All was going swimmingly until the privately owned Richardson Hotel Group fell into administration. Suddenly the collection of six individual establishments, situated in stunning locations on the South Devon and Cornwall coasts, with their striking period architecture, breathtaking views and award-winning dining, came under scrutiny from the taxman. Despite the setback, an ever-optimistic John commented at the time, 'This is just a glitch which will be sorted, I'm not worried. The company has plenty of assets and once two of them are sold, things will go back to normal.' By summer 2018, the Richardson Hotel Group was out of administration, but a certain John Burton-Race had walked out the door.

2

A CHANCE ENCOUNTER

RRIVING AT the Grand Hotel with its pleasant views across the bay, I decide to freshen up in the toilet … and promptly bump into John Burton-Race. Not quite the salubrious surroundings I had been anticipating for our first encounter. No matter. We wander to the comfortable lounge, where John orders a sparkling water. Americano and a sparkling water for me. Dressed casually in jeans and a loose sweater, John is taller than I had imaged, but that is television for you. He is also tanned, no doubt thanks in no small part to all that excellent warm sunshine and sea breeze he catches along this southern stretch of coastline. I had half expected him to be wearing chef's whites, snatching time to chat in between service. However, with time closing in on two o'clock, he is already looking a little battle weary. He tells me about the previous four hours of his exasperating morning, dealing with the minutiae that goes with his role: his head chef being a shit; a member of staff being caught on camera stealing; issues with the downstairs bakery; a meeting about how to open a bag of crisps; staff complaining about unemptied trash bins; paperwork … the list goes on. This when all he craves is to get his work clothes on and go in the kitchen where he can be left alone to do his thing. Having just put in a 70-hour week at 61 years of age and having only recently returned to kitchen duties after almost two years off for a series of illnesses, there is little wonder that family and friends constantly nag him about the fact that he works too hard but as he readily admits, he simply gets carried away. Managerial tasks frustrate the hell out of him when all he wants to be is creative. That passion has never wavered and is what has kept John Burton-Race at the top of his game in a culinary world constantly craving novelty and originality.

So here I am, seated next to a man about whom it has become conventional to think of as unpredictable, intense and prickly, a maverick performer constantly seeking perfection behind the scenes without compromise or conformity. There is a certainty about the rhetoric, because, clearly, he can be unpredictable, intense and prickly, but more often than not for good reason. For my part, I tend to take people at face value. So, going on first impressions, John Burton-Race comes across as disarmingly charming. Erudite, funny, thoughtful and at ease with himself and the occasion, he is eager to start the ball rolling. Without any prompting, he launches into a stream of anecdotes with no prior considered response to my first question. Momentarily caught off-guard, I suggest it might be appropriate to begin noting our conversation and he agrees. However, trying to get John Burton-Race to rewind when he is in fast-forward is an entirely different matter. It is easier to leave the tape running and for me to lock on to his orbit. Exuding a level of engaged charisma as he gushes forth with great waves of emotion, he is like a human Exocet on speed, circling and swooping in and out of childhood and growing up and school and safari holidays and bullying and cooking and family life. It is as if much of his past has been deliberately kept in mothballs in the bottom drawer; painful memories, hidden emotions, just waiting for the right moment for the release valve to blow. I sit quietly and listen attentively to a man so utterly complex and sensitive that it is hard to understand why he has often been criticised for his outward bullishness. But then, he is the first to put his hands up and admit to all those tirades that have brought him such bad press over the years: those days of anger and passion and pure creativity amid the daily grind of kitchen duty; those challenging, complex and toxic marital breakdowns that brought crushing lows in his life. No, John Burton-Race is never lost for words, and when he rolls into town, we have come to expect him to be still driven, still complex, still controversial, still living life at 100 miles an hour, still busying himself in the kitchen, still trying to exorcise his demons, and still happy to share a turbulent and endlessly fascinating life with anyone who cares—or dares—to listen. As I grow to know John Burton-Race better, and on a more personal level, I begin to slowly unravel the complexities of the man and a life comprising equal measures of brilliance and insecurity, self-deprecating charm and melancholic sufferance, and out of all that seeming negativity, one shining, defining characteristic: passion.

3

BABY STEPS

SINGAPORE, 1 May 1957. One of the hottest months of the year on the diamond-shaped island city-state located on the southern tip of the Malay Peninsula in southeast Asia. The second of the annual monsoon periods will launch itself on the heavily urbanised area in a matter of weeks, but the populace has other things on its mind. Even those who have made the journey to the south coast to embrace the beaches lining the Java Sea have their ears to the ground. For a momentous day is in the making, with the British Government due to change the course of history by agreeing to self-rule for the island colony. The Singapore Constitutional Conference had finally come to an end after weeks of intense talks between Chief Minister of Singapore Lim Yew Hock and Alan Lennox-Boyd, Secretary of State for the Colonies.

In another part of this constantly evolving city which former Chief Minister David Marshall famously called a 'pock-marked beauty shrouded in chloroform', a family is experiencing a different air of expectancy—the imminent birth of a baby boy. As May Day dawned, John William Burton-Race entered the world, the first child of Shirley and Cedric Keith Burton. The couple were childhood sweethearts, having met at Coalville Grammar School in Leicestershire. Keith went on to study geology at university in Nottingham. With a degree fresh in his back pocket, the couple married at Coalville Anglican Church and headed east to (then) Malaya in 1954, where Keith had secured a position as an Overseas Civil Servant seconded to the Malaysian Government. His principal job was exploring mineral deposits, a position which saw him travelling throughout Malaya's eleven provinces.

The Burtons found themselves near the capital of Ipoh in the second largest state of Batu Gajah, which literally translates as 'elephant stone'. Today, Ipoh is a thriving metropolis. It is divided into the Old Town, which nestles against a bend in the Kinta River, with its origins deeply rooted in the 19th century, the New Town, which spread during the 20th century and lies on the river's eastern bank, and the Newer Town, which sprawls out yet further east. With its signature dish of bean sprouts and chicken, Ipoh has found itself on the bucket list of many a tourist seeking an authentic culinary experience. There is a paradox at large here, because where the New Town is decidedly traditional in its table offerings, the Old Town steals a march in terms of trendy eateries. It is also where the British left a white-stucco legacy of colonial architecture and fashionable clubs. The Burtons were to spend a year in the town, settling into a comfortable existence before Keith was posted to the sleepy provincial town of Johor Bahru, which lies at the southern tip of the Malay Peninsula, opposite Singapore. Locals would travel the 16 miles to the popular island metropolis for shopping and dinner. When Shirley fell pregnant, tests revealed she had rhesus negative blood; fine with a first pregnancy but should a woman become pregnant a second time with a rhesus positive baby, her antibodies can attack the baby's red blood cells, which in turn can result in anemia and jaundice in the baby. With relatively limited medical facilities in their hometown, the couple availed themselves of the more complete and up-to-date expertise and services in Singapore.

Johor Bahru and Singapore are separated by the Johore Strait, a mile-wide arm of the South China Sea which had been dammed to form a causeway bearing road, rail and pedestrian links. The causeway leads into the 25km-long Bukit Timah Road, the longest road in Singapore, which in turn gives access to the commercial centre of Singapore. It was here that a suitably qualified doctor was contacted and consulted over several visits during Shirley's pregnancy. A pleasant nursing home was selected on Chancery Lane, just off Bukit Timah Road, in readiness for the birth. Much thought had been given to the baby's name, and it was eventually agreed that should it be a boy, he would be named John William after his paternal great-grandfather. As for a girl, the name eluded Keith when I spoke to him about it.

The prospective parents lived in what can best be described as an upmarket housing estate for colonial civil servants, which was all very chummy and agreeable. Surrounded by an extensive lawn, the two-storey property was sizeable enough to warrant Keith to employ the services of two Malay maids to take care of domestic chores. The nearest neighbours enhanced their early mornings with birdsong—sounds emanating from two cages with their pretty-coloured birds. Whenever the neighbours went away, the birds would be entrusted to other occupants of the estate. So, it was on one fine day in April that the Burtons found themselves with some flapping lodgers.

Come the evening of April 30, Shirley was feeling decidedly off-colour and retired early. As her pain worsened, the penny eventually dropped. Keith grabbed the pre-packed bag, telephoned the nursing home and with his wife on board, drove hell for leather along Bukit Timah Road in his modest Standard 8 motorcar, which had been purchased with a loan from the British Government. It was one of only 50,000 motor vehicles in the whole of Malaya at the time.

In the small hours of May Day 1957, John William was born. Leaving his wife with their born son, an exhausted but extremely proud Keith returned home—only to discover that the caged birds had taken flight. With the household routinely pampered by two maidservants, the date also happened to be a Muslim holiday, the Islamic equivalent of Christmas, and the maids were on leave, so the house stood empty.

After five days, staff at the nursing home had suffered enough of baby John's constant exercising of his lungs, begging Shirley to take him home. 'My mother always told me she was given the wrong child, firstly because I was terribly ugly and secondly because I was a complete pain in the arse!' John tells me.

Baby John was to spend many an hour travelling around the provinces in his father's car. There was, however, a downside, as the vehicle had no air-conditioning or interior fan, and the only cooling device available to the occupants was stifling warm air passing through the open windows. In those early days, John travelled in a large rattan bassinet and to get in and out of the car, it was necessary to incline the carrier at 45 degrees. When he could eventually sit up, one of his favourite pastimes from his rear seat was to meticulously unpick the sewing on the upholstery.

At home, John continued to make his presence felt. If his demands were not met or if he felt they were insufficient for his needs, he would yell at the top of his voice, which was all very well when he wanted to express himself but it also led to a hernia. At six months old, he found himself confined to bed in Johor Bahru General Hospital. Taking an instant dislike to all that went on around him, including the attendant doctor and the food, he continued to yell, which resulted in his stitches bursting, so it was back to the operating theatre once again. The traumatic events took their toll on Shirley and her nervousness was having an adverse effect on her son, so she returned to the family home and left Keith to hospital duties.

4

MALAY MALAISE

FATE, IT must be said, on occasion can deal an extraordinary hand. Prior to meeting with John's father at his Leicestershire home, where I was gathering background material for this biography, Keith Burton and his third wife Suryati had been busy sorting through years of accumulated family possessions in preparation for a permanent move back to their home in Indonesia. Buried among the jumble of monochrome family photographs were several yellowing, typewritten sheets of paper. It transpired that Shirley had planned on documenting her early life in the Far East. Written from their home at 2000 Jalan Larkin, Johor Bahru, the notes reveal in intimate detail her innermost thoughts on her early and clearly fraught experiences of motherhood. The first two foolscap sheets are headlined, in capital letters, 'SOME MOTHER'S HAVE THEM'.

The text reads as follows (I have taken the liberty of altering the spelling and punctuation, where necessary): 'I decided before having my children that I would bring them up by the book. What I didn't reckon on were the children. When John was born he drove us all mad demanding food from morning till night, despite THE BOOK'S assurance that he would only need food every four hours, so, in desperation, when he was six weeks old I gave him some solid food. I half expected him to explode, but after six weeks of practically no sleep I didn't really care if he did. However, he took to eating as if that was all he was born for, which I later learned was quite true, and almost swallowed the spoon in his eagerness never to leave anything, whether he liked it or not. After we had ironed out that little difficulty and had fed the Brute, we found that something else was worrying him. He would writhe and contort in his pram and eventually I decided, after searching in vain through THE BOOK, that he was trying to sit up. And, sure enough, as soon as he was successful, we had three peaceful days. It took him that long to realise that he had no independent method of propulsion. So, he tried to crawl. He started by rocking on his knees, then after a while he would set off at a great rate ... backwards. However, he soon got fore and aft sorted out, and then, of course, he just had to walk ... and walk he did at the age of ten months, and two months later his sister, Clare, was born.'

To Shirley's relief, the town of Ipoh proved to be a thriving metropolis with numerous shops and two large department stores. Clearly not knowing what to expect from her move to Asia, she wrote another faded document head-lined 'FIRST IMPRESSIONS', unearthed by Keith during his house clearance and to whom I remain grateful for allowing me to reproduce the contents. 'From the aeroplane, Malaya appeared to be one mass of unpenetrated jungle. Occasionally white threads of rivers were to be seen, but it wasn't until we were actually circling the small airfield that any sign of human activity was evident. I wasn't expected to live in a tree after all, and so far, there was no sign of the dreaded Communists whom I had expected to see hiding behind every coconut tree.' Shirley was entranced by the different races, her favourite being the beautiful and delicate Chinese women in their lovely form-fitting cheongsams, although the Indian girls wearing flowing and graceful saris and the Malay in colourful sarongs also had a definite appeal.

Worried that she would not understand the language, Shirley busied herself with a Teach Yourself Malay book and managed quite well. The local cuisine also proved to be a factor in her induction to Malay life. She noted, 'As a new arrival I found that everyone thought it was their duty to introduce me to the local curry, which I found virtually un-eatable. Later I was to prefer it to any other food. My first attempt at eating Chinese style wasn't an overwhelming success either. I loved the delicious, spicy flavours but found the chopsticks a little difficult to manipulate, but even that came in time.'

Invited to the house of a Sikh family for dinner, the Burtons spent an entertaining two hours wrapping curried fish in chapattis, which Shirley described as 'pancake-like things, made with flour and water', and eating them with their fingers. 'So much easier than chopsticks!' she wrote. 'The climax of the evening came after we had finished the curry, when our host appeared with a pie dish of alarming proportions, and in it a rice pudding, which his English textbooks had assured him we ate. Unable to visualise anyone enjoying a rice pudding as such, he had made it more interesting by the addition of large amounts of peanuts, bananas, raisins and papaya. I am still wondering how I managed to eat it all. Probably because my host and hostess were looking on with such obvious pride.'

During the time of Keith Burton's appointment, government servants on overseas duties were entitled to four days' home leave for each month of service. This leave was much coveted, especially when there was the possibility of extending the period back home if the employee happened to enroll on a course deemed to add value to their job. With John approaching 10 months old, the Burtons decided it was time to sojourn on home turf. With the option of travelling either by sea or air, the couple felt that a sea voyage, however pleasant and tempting the opportunity might have been, would be a step too far, bearing in mind their son's fiery temperament, so they opted instead for a British Airways flight. True to form, John was inconsolable on the plane and happy to let the world know of his discomfort. While mum and dad tried to placate their son with an assortment of milk, bananas and chocolate, the stewardesses rather sensibly decided to give him a wide berth. This resulted in his parents assembling a small pile of leftovers. Having stuffed the ashtrays to overflowing, Keith decided the best course of action would be to eat any leftovers himself.

Having arrived back safely in the UK, Keith's first port of call was the local garage, where he ordered a new Ford Consul, to be shipped out to the Far East for his personal use; another privilege of being an overseas civil servant. John had been quiet during most of the transaction. However, having grown accustomed to the weather in Asia, he was not overly impressed with the Shetland Wool jumpsuit he had been forced to wear, clearly troubled by the restrictions afforded by the arms and legs. With his son screaming objections, Keith was unable to hear all the instructions offered to him about the car's heating system, resulting in a chilly drive to Coalville in Leicestershire. Seeking respite from their child's continuous vocal dexterity, John was immediately placed in the care of his maternal grandparents, a move that, according to Keith, suited all parties. Being the first grandson, John was happy to soak up all the pampering. In the meantime, Keith managed to extend his leave by taking a technical course in Aberystwyth.

It was in Wales that John's sister Clare was born, on April 22, 1958, a few days before her brother's first birthday. Shirley later noted: 'This is where we begin again, I thought, and swiftly put aside THE BOOK. But, first of all Clare liked to sleep and sleep and she would, no matter where she was or went. Her last consideration was feeding, and she obviously thought the whole business was rather a bore. She had no intention of ever sitting up until in desperation I plonked her on her bottom when she was six months old, and there she sat. She could do it all the time!! Neither would she crawl. If she thought there was something worth her notice in the vicinity, she would use all her feminine wiles to get it, and would only fetch it herself if absolutely necessary, which wasn't often. She was definitely born with a silver spoon in her mouth, but someone had definitely put it there for her.'

Concerned that their son had been spoiled in Johor Bahru, and now here he was in Leicestershire receiving similar treatment from his doting grandparents, the Burtons decided to return to Malaya after Keith finished his course, with the intention of instilling some level of discipline into their son. The best laid plans, and all that. Within weeks, they had sent a telegram to the children's grandmother, Irene Manning, asking if she could fly out for a holiday—the ulterior motive being for her to act as temporary housekeeper, a position she was to manage most effectively. Keith recalls that John was particularly well behaved during his christening at St Andrew's Cathedral in Singapore. As it transpired, the Bishop of Singapore, Robin Woods, had been a parish priest at their Leicestershire village. The Bishop was later to become Chaplain to Her Majesty, Queen Elizabeth II.

From a very early age, John formed a particularly close bond with his sister, who had been born two months prematurely. Clare was such a tiny bundle that John nicknamed her Diddy. As she was unable to suckle properly, her mother resorted to force-feeding her by spoon. It was discovered early on that Clare was lactose intolerant, and the family spent hours coercing her to eat. As long as it was some form of pudding, she was fine. The concerned big brother once even convinced his little sister to eat a scorpion! 'Try this, Diddy,' was his favourite saying. John's preference was for chocolate and the more the better. It was a love he adopted from Grandpa Burton, himself a chocoholic. It wasn't unknown for a young John to consume seven Easter eggs at a time—before lunch. Grandpa Burton truly loved his grandchildren and would often take John to watch Leicester City whenever the family was in England. He was a wonderful pianist and a great prankster, and one of his favourite pastimes was to hide treats in the pantry for the children to find. The children were devastated when he passed away aged only 52.

Back in Singapore, the Burtons enjoyed all the trappings that came with being a part of the colonial set, with servants, a chauffeur and the occasional helicopter to ferry the family around. John recalls his mother driving a red open-top MG F with wire wheels, enjoying all the glamour that her position afforded her while his father worked hard and kept the money rolling in. Fine, you might think, except that John was to later become the victim of a dysfunctional household devoid of both love and homeliness. After a further two-and-a half years in Malaya, serious cracks were showing in his parents' relationship.

'All I can remember about the house in Malaya was that it had flame trees at the bottom of the garden and monkeys which jumped from the flame trees into a little stream,' says John. 'I used to sit as a two or three-year-old with my Alsatian dog waiting for them to jump into the water to cool themselves, and then send my Alsatian in to catch them. I got up to all sorts of things. I was probably one of those children who caused their parents a lot of grief and I think, had they had the opportunity, they would have swapped me for anything. In hindsight, I didn't seem to have a lot in common with them anyway.'

By the time the family returned to England for their second spell of leave in 1962, with John approaching his fifth birthday, the marriage had broken down irrevocably. Keith purchased a house for the family in Appleby Magna, near Measham in Leicestershire, and returned to Malaya alone. The break-up had a knock-on effect for Keith, who had fallen victim to tropical neurasthenia, a condition characterised by physical and mental exhaustion and often associated with depression or emotional stress, in a similar vein to chronic fatigue syndrome. That early, shattered relationship with his natural father was to cause John endless distress in later life. 'I loved him. I hated him. Felt rejected by him. I felt a need to prove something to him,' he told The Guardian newspaper in 2008.

5

INNER DEMONS

Shirley Burton took the break-up of her marriage extremely badly and suffered serious bouts of depression. 'All I used to think about was where my father was, but never asked,' John tells me. 'I can recall that it was always on my mind that he was missing. Something else that always occurred to me was how upset, constantly depressed and sad and in all sorts of a mess my mother was. There were times when I was frightened for her. There were times when she attempted to take her own life because of her depression. It turned out that my father had obviously disappointed her and, having been childhood sweethearts, the fact that their relationship had broken down practically destroyed her.'

With his mother either taking to her bed for days on end or lying on the couch in the front room staring into vacant space and not wanting to move, let alone care for her children, John would often hide underneath the couch, imagining he was protecting her, perhaps from her inner demons. Mother and son would eventually fall asleep in front of the flickering screen of the black and white television which sat atop the coffee table. It was a desperate

31

period for the children, who at one stage had been told that their father was dead. With Shirley's mental health in freefall, they would be left to fend for themselves for days on end. On one occasion, they cut out butterflies from rolls of wallpaper and plastered them all over the house. Come breakfast each morning, John would prepare his sister a bowl of cereals while he indulged in his passion for chocolate.

John learned from an early age that cooking was not necessarily about how complicated a dish might be to make it special, but rather what ingredients were used. Fresh in-season raspberries drizzled with lavender honey and a dollop of crème fraiche … a tomato salad picked from the vine, turned a beautiful shade of red from plenty of sunshine and water … a drizzle of golden olive oil, sea salt and basil — simple, yet defining moments for a young, aspiring cook.

Behind their small cottage was a field where sheep would occasionally graze. It was also where five-year-old John took himself off on one of his mini adventures, hunting for large mushrooms. Brushing away the early-morning dew, he would smell them and think how wonderful they were. One day, during one of his mother's rare lucid periods, he asked her what he could do with the mushrooms. Shirley told her son how to make a mushroom omelette. 'To this day, I can still remember that omelette and how brilliant it was to create something from next to nothing to eat,' he says. 'I thought it was spectacular — not because I was a genius cook but because the eggs were from the chickens free ranging in front of the cottage and the mushrooms were from the field. It was simply me and a frying pan.' A fussy Clare refused to eat the omelette because it had turned almost black from the ink of the mushrooms which had leaked out into the egg when John was cooking it. He was happy with the result though and can still recall the sense of accomplishment. 'Thinking about cooking, you start with an empty pan and from simple ingredients you make something, sometimes from very little. Even today, I often wonder if there is as creative a job as being a chef. I love it and always have done.' John would later include a recipe for the humble omelette in First Crack Your Egg!, the book he co-authored with celebrated chef Angela Hartnett and written to accompany the popular television series Kitchen Criminals.

OMELETTE
(Serves 1)

Ingredients

3 eggs
10g cold butter, diced
2 tsp oil
Salt and pepper

Method

1. Crack the eggs into a bowl and beat with a fork until smooth. Stir in the cold, diced butter.
2. Heat a heavy non-stick frying pan over a high heat and add the oil.
3. Season the eggs with salt and pepper. When the oil is smoking-hot, pour the eggs quickly into the pan.
4. Using a fork in a circular motion, move the contents of the pan round and round, while at the same time moving the pan back and forth across the heat. Allow the eggs to start coagulating.
5. Stop stirring and shaking the pan. Allow the eggs to form a light skin, and then remove the pan from the heat.
6. Pick up the pan and tilt the handle upwards and away from you. At the same time, tap the handle of the pan so that the omelette moves towards the opposite end of the pan.
7. Using the side of a fork, fold the omelette over to form a cigar shape.
8. Turn the pan over and tip the omelette on to a plate. Serve immediately.

With his mother on a daily cocktail of anti-depressants, John continued to take on the role of man about the house. 'It was a bit silly really, but there wasn't anyone else.' One of the chores he took on board was the shopping. While Shirley was lying heavily sedated on the couch, John would take money from her purse and walk down the hill along a country lane to the grocers, where he would ask what could be purchased for the change in his pocket. On one occasion he spied what looked to him like massive cabbages. Not knowing exactly what they were and because they were so cheap, he bought one. A proud John presented his mother with the purchase, only to be scolded and told that he had, in fact, bought a cow cabbage, normally fed to cattle, rabbits, goats and sheep for their high-quality nutrients and because they are easily digestible. The family ended up eating cow cabbage every day for a week, cooked every which way possible. 'It was really, really awful, and I burnt myself for the first time trying to cook it. It wasn't pleasant, and certainly not for my mother,' he recalls.

The family lived close to a butcher's shop, where John and Clare would occasionally be invited for a meal in the company of the couple's ferocious dog. John recalls the butcher's wife making delicious faggots served with rich gravy, which they sold in the shop.

John also has fond memories of the fish and chip shop van which would call by on a Friday. Because he had no money for himself, he would be told by the owner to wait at the side of the vehicle until all the customers had been served. Then all the bits of battered fish that had broken off in the fryer would be scraped together, placed in a paper cone and handed to the appreciative youngster. John would smother them in salt and vinegar and think he was in heaven. It was those early food moments that laid the foundation stones for his chosen career.

Beryl Manning, the youngest of seven children and sister to John's grand-mother Irene, recalls her nephew as being 'the loveliest little boy'. When the family was living in their cottage in Appleby Magna, Auntie Beryl resided in Ibstock eight miles away. She was always available to lend a hand, sewing the children's names in their school clothes, doing the washing and helping clean of the cottage. With the families living in such close proximity, Beryl's daughter Yvonne occasionally acquired Clare's cast-off clothing.

For transport, Shirley would fetch Beryl in her Bubble car. Designed in the early 1950s during a time of austerity after the Second World War, these iconic means of transport were a cheap, radical alternative to more conventional vehicles. With such limited space available to passengers, John and Clare would sit on the floor of the vehicle. Clare recalls her mother's erratic driving, often taking corners on two wheels. Considering that the vehicle only had three wheels in the first place, it was not the most sensible way to drive, and possibly accounts for the fact that on one occasion Clare actually fell out! It was all very much a family affair, with Beryl's brother Douglas modernising the house while her husband Walter built a garage. There were certainly good times and fun times, but on the flip side there were the occasions when Shirley was suffering from those serious bouts of depression. She would shout, not only at the children but also at Beryl. 'Although I loved her, she was always bossy, even with me, but I used to be able to give it her back. I know she was very much in love with Keith, and things started to go wrong for her when he left and returned to Kuala Lumpur.'

Even at such a tender age, it was clear to Beryl that her nephew had leanings towards cookery. 'He would say to me, "Auntie Beryl, do you want a cream cake making?" It was lovely. He always wanted to be in the kitchen doing things. When his career took off and I saw him on television, I was so proud of him.'

I was extremely saddened to learn that Beryl passed away in early 2019, not long after we had spent a pleasant afternoon together in the company of Clare and Yvonne.

The following is the recipe Irene passed on to him when he was small. He admits to having been known to eat so much of it that he felt physically sick! He also admits defeat when perfecting this cake, as Grandma would always make a better version of it.

GRANDMOTHER'S CAKE
(Serves 6)

Ingredients

225g plain flour

½ tsp baking powder

275g natural glacé cherries, quartered

115g ground almonds

225g caster sugar

225g unsalted butter, softened

4 eggs, at room temperature

Grated zest and juice of 1 lemon

12 sugar cubes, coarsely crushed

Method

1. Preheat the oven to 180°C/350°F/Gas 4.

2. Line a 20cm round cake tin with greaseproof paper or baking parchment.

3. Sift the flour and baking powder into a bowl. In a separate bowl, toss the cherries with the ground almonds. In another mixing bowl, add the sugar and butter, and beat together until pale and fluffy. Add the flour and slowly beat the eggs, one at a time. Stop the food mixer and carefully fold in the cherries and almonds by hand. Sprinkle in a little lemon juice and zest.

4. Spoon the mixture into the cake tin and, using a spatula, level off the top. Sprinkle with the crushed sugar cubes and bake in the oven for 1 hour, then cover with a sheet of brown paper or foil and continue to bake for a further 30 minutes or until the cake has shrunk away from the sides. Leave to cool in the tin for about 15 minutes before turning out on a wire rack to cool completely.

Store in an airtight container for one or two days before eating to allow the cake to mature and moisten.

6

CHANGING PALATES

A s shirley slowly recovered from her bouts of depression, she began dating Dennis Race, a friend of Keith's. John recalls of his stepfather, 'He did something which catapulted his career and that was the pinnacle, a civil engineer working for a local company to this big-shot who had written a paper about designing a road from Thailand to Burma, some of it following an old war road, blowing up and drilling mountains to get a road through, and it made him successful.'

That success landed Dennis employment with the United Nations as Director of Development and Planning for the Far East. Once settled in Thailand, the Races had to find an appropriate school for their children. It came in the form of the American School of Bangkok, which offered an American curriculum with an international perspective. Thanks to its rigorous teaching programme, today it is recognised as one of the top international schools in Thailand, with many of its students receiving academic scholarships at some of the world's top universities, including Harvard, University of California, Berkeley, University of Washington and the University of Tokyo.

It was into this alien world of prestigious academia that young John and Clare were thrust.

A shy, retiring child and lazy too, with little interest in the curriculum and zero acumen for sport, John's curiosity sometimes got the better of him. 'I remember being scared of heights. There was this swimming pool, and one day I decided to climb up the concrete platform. I was terrified. You could not pull me off the railings because I was clinging on so tightly. Once I had reached the uppermost platform, I looked down and saw all these people around the pool looking up at me. I felt that the humiliation of having to try and clamber back down was probably worse than the fear of jumping. My mother was shouting, telling me not to be so stupid and to climb down immediately. Instead I ignored her, stood on the edge…and jumped. I knew then that I was totally out of control, but the feeling was somehow amazing. I just reasoned, "I can't do anything about this". The fall felt like the world had gone into slow motion and then, bang, I hit the water.' John landed badly, hitting the bottom of the pool, which resulted in him chipping a tooth and piercing his lip. There was blood everywhere. However, instead of crying and running to his mother, a defiant John Burton-Race ran back to the platform and repeated the stunt. After hitting the water for a second time, he rose to the surface, only to find his mother staring down at him and berating him for his utter stupidity. In later life, Shirley told her son that he always jumped into things without thinking. 'I suppose that is down to my being an emotional person, and often out of control,' he says. 'I love Thailand. I kept snakes and we had two runty dogs, one called Dam, the other Rons (Damrons being a very bad Thai expletive), and a big mongrel called Fairy. With maids and cooks in the household, I enjoyed learning how to prepare several Thai dishes from the kitchen staff. Whenever the opportunity arose, I would visit the local food markets, taking a keen interest in all the tropical fruits and fish. I experienced local food, went to the jungle and ate local fayre, slept wherever we were in the countryside and as far as I was concerned, as a young child it was like a safari. I was already really very passionate by then about cooking.'

CHICKEN CURRY
(Serves 8)

Ingredients

2 x 1.5kg chickens, each cut into 8 pieces

4 tbsp vegetable oil

3 onions, chopped

1 apple (Bramley or Granny Smith), peeled and finely diced

3 garlic cloves, peeled and chopped

20g raw stem ginger, peeled and finely chopped

2 red peppers, seeded and diced

2 green peppers, seeded and diced

1 tbsp tomato purée

1 tsp cumin powder

15g mild (Korma) curry powder or paste

20g hot (Madras) curry powder or paste

1 cinnamon stick

400ml coconut milk

1 tbsp mango chutney

500ml chicken stock

1.4kg small King Edward potatoes, peeled

Method

1. Preheat the oven to 220°C/425°F/Gas 7.

2. Heat a large frying pan. Add half the vegetable oil and fry half of the chicken to a golden-brown colour; this will take about 10 minutes. With a slotted spoon, transfer the pieces to a colander placed over a bowl to drain off any excess fat. Repeat with the other chicken pieces.

3. Put a large saucepan on the stove to heat and add the remaining vegetable oil. As soon as it starts to smoke, add the onions, apple, garlic, ginger and peppers. Cook for about 5 minutes over a high heat, stirring all the time. Stir in the tomato purée and cook for a further 2 minutes.

4. Add the cumin and both the curry powders or pastes. Stir the ingredients regularly so that they do not catch or burn. Add the cinnamon stick. Pour in the coconut milk and bring to the boil, stirring as you do so. Add the mango chutney. Pour in the chicken stock and bring the sauce back up to the boil. With a ladle, skim off any surfacing scum or foam and discard.

5. Add the chicken pieces and cover the saucepan with a lid. Put it in the oven and cook for 20 minutes.

6. Remove the curry from the oven. Give it a stir, add the potatoes, and return to the oven for a further 30 minutes. Remove the curry from the oven and serve.

You can garnish the curry with a Malaysian-style sambal: roasted peanuts in their skins, sliced banana, boiled egg quarters, red onion rings, mango chutney and sliced fresh tomatoes. Serve with plain boiled basmati rice or an unpolished Thai variety and Naan Bread. John likes to make the curry the day before serving, because as with a lot of casserole-type dishes, it always tastes better re-heated, and if left for a day or two, the aromas have more time to flavour the meat and sauce.

For John, the excitement of something new offers the best buzz possible, and even today likens this feeling to his work in the kitchen. 'If I do a dish under the right circumstances and where money is no object, and I can be as creative and expansive as I like to make something beautiful, I will do it once, or perhaps twice, and I then won't do it again. It is that freedom of not being controlled by anything or anyone, of not being frustrated by any restrictions, when I feel I can be at my creative best. If I teach you how to cook and you are an amazing copier, you will get 90 per cent out of my 100. If you then teach your junior, he will get 80 per cent. When, a week later, your creativity has gone full circle and the dish comes back to you, you suddenly don't recognise it. It is almost like a kind of insanity, whereby I am totally driven, and cannot stand second best in anything.'

Like her brother, Clare has fond memories of their time in Bangkok. Even at such a tender age, she soaked up the culture and enjoyed spending time at school with her American friends. She also remembers a wonderful

Christmas holiday in Chiang Mai. Home to elaborate Buddhist temples, the city is situated in the mountainous north of Thailand, and it was here that the family spent time with the elephants.

Street food, curries, noodles, chillis… nothing was off the menu for a curious John and Clare, whose palates were changing quite markedly. The household chefs would cook European food because they presumed that was what the family would want to eat. With their penchant for local food, however, the youngsters often sneaked into the kitchen after consuming a three-course lunch and eat what the servants had cooked for themselves. It was a habit they were to repeat while living in Indonesia. John's enthusiasm for cooking and experimenting with different flavours was evident from the age of five when he and Clare would have competitions to see who could make the best cakes. John would make a delicious chocolate cake and Clare would attempt a rock cake but wrongly add mixed herbs instead of mixed spice. Clare's bumbling in the kitchen became a running joke, particularly with John and Grandma Irene. For John, it was always about the ingredients, and for as long as Clare could remember he was always the perfectionist in the kitchen. John's early love of food was also evidenced when he and his sister would travel to and from Thailand as unaccompanied minors. While Clare would try and sleep her way through the long-haul BOAC flight, John would order from the menu, waking his sister up to a pile of food in front of her.

'We had cooks for nearly all of my childhood and I learnt very quickly the difference between food prepared by an accomplished local cook, using fresh local ingredients, and the unambitious food we are sometimes subjected to in England,' he tells me. 'Growing up and going to school in Thailand, I liked nothing better than fresh papaya with a little lime squeezed all over it for my daily breakfast. Heaven for me was noodles with prawns or duck from the street sellers who would stand at the entrances to the food markets. There are hundreds of different types of rice, all with different flavours, just as we have hundreds of different varieties of potatoes in England.' For John to pick just one dish from this period in his life is impossible, although one of his favourites remains Yam Yam Goong.

YAM YAM GOONG

Ingredients

1 lemon grass
2 garlic cloves
30g galangal
20g fresh ginger
½ tsp chilli powder
250g tomatoes, skinned and de-seeded
250g shiitaki mushrooms
125g shallots
500g large prawns (shelled with their tails on)
Juice of 2 small limes
5 tbsp nam pla
1 tsp light soy sauce
1 bunch of small leaf Thai basil and fresh coriander

Method

1. Crush the lemon grass. Slice the galangal and ginger. Peel and crush the garlic to a paste. Slice and add the shallots.
2. Fry together over a gentle heat in a little light oil. Add the chilli powder. Pour in the stock and bring it to the boil. Turn down to a simmer for 10 minutes.
3. Add the skinned, quartered tomatoes, and wash and slice the mushrooms, and add them to the soup. Add the prawns. Cook for a further 5 minutes.
4. Remove the pan from the stove, season with lime juice and nam pla.
5. Serve the Thai basil and fresh coriander.

7

LOITERING IN A BUBBLE

UPON RETURNING to the UK, the family relocated to Sarisbury Green, situated roughly halfway between Southampton and Fareham on the Hampshire coast. With excellent schools and affordable housing, the village has always been popular with families, with plenty of surrounding countryside for outdoor activities. It was not long before things in the household took a sudden and devastating turn for the children. One morning, having risen at the crack of dawn, John watched through his bedroom window in Woodlands Close as his mother and stepfather climbed into a taxi and drove away. They had not gone shopping. Rather, the couple were headed for Indonesia, where Dennis Race had been offered a new position. No explanation to their children, no heartfelt goodbyes, nothing—just gone, the taxi's rear lights flickering and gradually fading into the distance. Heartbroken and feeling psychologically alone, John sobbed uncontrollably for a week. Even with Clare by his side, the rejection felt complete. 'I thought, I am just going to walk up that road, and in the morning, they are going to come for me. I found out later that my mother had decided that the best way for her and my stepfather to get on in life was to leave us behind to attend the local primary school while her new husband could pursue his career, wherever that may have taken them,' he tells me. The alienation was not so complete for Clare, who admits to never having bonded completely with her mother. In fact, Shirley was quite happy to tell her daughter, 'I don't love you because you are too like your father.' Clare remembers when she was about seven, her mother would leave suicide letters around the house which she would discover and read. 'Whether or not she left those letters for me to find deliberately, I don't know. They would state that if her husband did not do as he was told, she would kill herself. I don't think she ever had a great relationship with my stepfather.'

The immediate family only became aware of the children's plight when an uncle chanced by the house and found them home alone. Clare and John were placed with neighbours, a move that had devastating results and left both children mentally scarred. On one occasion, desperate for the attention of other family members, the children sneaked out of the house and phoned Grandma Manning, pleading with her to collect them and take them home with her. Unfortunately, it was not to be. Despite the setback, John has a true fondness for his grandmother. 'She was always wonderful to me. I was her favourite, which was great, because I had never been anyone's favourite before and I could do no wrong, despite what my mother may have thought. Having said that, I can't say I had a terribly hard background. Emotionally, yes, mentally, definitely, but looking back there was nothing like six in a bed and a front room full of relations. It just wasn't like that.'

Irene Manning was a simple, homely cook who never wrote anything down properly. 'She made this wonderful fruitcake using half margarine and half lard. I have never been able to make it successfully the way she did. Every time I attempt it, I take it out of the oven thinking it is cooked and it sinks in the middle. It drives me mad! She would try and explain the process to me, and I would listen to her over and over again. I begged her for years to write the recipe down, but I don't think she could because she never weighed anything. She also made the most wonderful biscuits and jams.' Irene was also fond of making pickles, whether it be with onions, beetroot or piccalilli. Then there was lemon curd, amazing steamed puddings, egg custards, beef dumplings and apple dumplings, often created in competition with her sister Beryl. 'She would make absolutely everything, and was a lovely, kind and gentle person. Because she never wrote anything down, the only recipes I have are the ones that I took down when watching her cook. Her scone recipe was very special. I've eaten hundreds of them with her homemade plum and strawberry jam.'

PLAIN SCONES
(Add 125g sultanas and/or raisins for fruit scones)

Ingredients
- 1kg plain flour
- 125g caster sugar
- 50g baking powder
- 125g butter
- 600ml milk
- 1 egg (for wash)

Method
1. Preheat oven to 220 °F.
2. Sieve the flour in a large bowl. Add the sugar and baking powder and add the butter to form a crumb.
3. With a fork, vigorously stir in the milk until the dough comes together. Don't over-mix the dough.
4. Dust a work surface with a little flour and turn out the dough. Cut into two pieces and gently roll and shape until it looks like a fat rolling pin.
5. Cut the scones 1 inch thick and lay them down on a baking sheet.
6. Beat the egg and gently brush the tips of the scones with a little egg. Cook them in batches.
7. When cooked, risen and golden brown, turn them out on to rack to cool. When cold, the remainder can be frozen.

The neighbours with whom the children were living were never much into cooking proper meals, either for their own children or for John and Clare, so John used the opportunity to prepare what Clare describes as whole meals, including Sunday lunch. On occasional weekends they would visit one of the grandmothers of their new, temporary family who would produce smoked oysters, which intrigued John no end.

Attending the local primary school, the children always found dinner times exciting and not a little entertaining. Clare recalls the time they were treated to curry for lunch. None of their fellow pupils had the slightest idea what the dish was. Having devoured curries on a regular basis in Thailand, they managed to put away seven dinners and seven puddings in one sitting, with John forever saying to sister Diddy, 'Try this one.'

When I tactfully return to the subject of John's mother and his relationship with her, our conversation turns darker and I sense the cracks appearing in his psyche. Clearly devoid of love and affection he earnestly craved, and which was particularly evidenced after Shirley re-married, it was as if the circle of alienation was complete.

Just like his earliest childhood memories are a pile of mismatched fragments, so, too, John's adult life has proven to be one of misunderstanding. I doubt anyone has referred to John Burton-Race as melancholic before. Part of me believes he is, preferring as he does to remain on the outside, where he feels most comfortable, finding solace when he has order in his life, with little or no time for compromise. It is as if he is loitering in a bubble where that order is a protective veil and he can find some meaning in his life. Then he is suddenly off again, rarely finishing one sentence before launching into another, his mind a scattergun of remembrances and emotions.

John's parents had rented out their house in Woodlands Close and upon returning to the UK, they took up residence again for a brief spell before returning for a second tour in Indonesia, this time taking the children with them. Aged ten, John was to find favour with the family's chef in Jakarta. He remembers making 'a sort of Malaysian curry, which is lighter and cleaner. It is all about texture and different tones of flavours, much more so than Indian food. In Indian cooking you don't have the sambal, which could be roasted peanuts, slices of cucumber, raw red onion, a slice of banana and tomato, which could then be accompanied by some red curried duck eggs. You take a portion of rice and a portion of curry, and then sprinkle all these things on top. It sounds a bit odd, but it really works. To this day, I can still taste those fantastic flavours.'

8

KITE FIGHTS AND
FIERY CHILLIES

Iᴛ ᴡᴀꜱ while living in Fareham in 1965 that John's half-sister Rebecca
was born to Shirley and Dennis Race. At the time, John's stepfather
was working in a consultancy capacity, advising on civil and agricul-
tural engineering projects for the Louis Berger Group (now part of WSP).
With Dennis's schedule taking him from the Far East to the Middle East and
Africa, the children made the most of their holidays, particularly when they
found themselves in Bandung, the capital of West Java Province. Set amid
volcanoes and tree plantations, they enjoyed the art of kite fighting, when
kites are launched from a divided field. The kites would be equipped with
bamboo hooks in the line called jam pa. As the kites engaged, they would
become entangled and the winner was the one who managed to drag the
opponent's kite into their field. John and Clare could not have been living
in a more perfect spot in order to pursue this long-standing tradition, as the
north-eastern monsoon winds which blow from inland southward to the Thai
Gulf from February until November are known as the kite wind. As the cool

dry air passes through the north and northeastern part of the country, rice farmers would traditionally gather in open grounds to fly their kites at night after a long day's harvest.

John enjoyed hours of fun kite fighting with children from the village in the valley below his home. Every time he ventured out with one of his colourful kites, the village kids would try to cut his kite down or allow the kites to become entangled before attempting to take his kite as the prize. After losing several kites, John became much better at the game, thanks in no small part to the head gardener. Using thin cotton for the string, he would grind up broken glass bottles and mix with cochineal and paper glue. The line would then be passed through the glass dust. The final phase was to bake the line in the sun. John's pride and joy was a Garuda made of rice paper and bamboo, with spectacular colours and a 15-foot tale. A Garuda has been described as the king of birds, with its kite-like figure normally shown in zoomorphic form (a giant bird with partially open wings) or an anthropomorphic form (a man with wings and bird features). It is part of the state insignia in Thailand, Myanmar, Cambodia and Indonesia. One day, within minutes of his kite becoming airborne, three smaller kites attacked it. John fought off one by cutting the line. The second he hauled in and kept as a prize before attacking the third kite. The battle lasted a good three hours. Those hours spent learning about the wind and how to control the kite proved invaluable. As he was packing up his kite, one of the village boys asked if he would like to go to his house for something to eat. Upon arrival, the child set up a charcoal fire and placed a dirty-looking wok on top. His family grew potatoes as a staple crop. Once dug up, they were cleaned and dried in the sun in their husks for two days, before being podded. The youngster then put peanut oil in the wok and added a handful of shelled peanuts, and when the wok was smoking, threw in unbleached sea salt. He then fired tiny, fiery hot chillies called chavee. For John, it was an amazing experience and a taste sensation like nothing he had ever experienced. With their bright, maroon-coloured skins and crispy golden-brown inners, and hot to the point that they almost blistered his lips, they were crisp, crunchy, and gorgeous.

Rebecca remembers with fondness their time spent in Bandung. 'We had a fabulous house. I don't know how my parents swung it, but the property belonged to a member of the Royal Family. Apparently, it had been gifted to a princess as a wedding present. It came with an enormous amount of land, plus a deer which drank beer and a monkey which, although tethered to a tree, could run around the garden. We also had a resident buffalo. I remember once it got into the house and left a massive parcel. After that episode, it was shipped off to a farm.' On one of Shirley's visits to the UK from Bandung, she took John and Clare with her. They were to be schooled in England and live with Grandma Manning. Being so much younger, Rebecca stayed with her parents. It would not be until much later in life that the children re-established contact with their father, Keith Burton.

John loved living in Bandung. 'Geographically it's beautiful, being very mountainous with steep, terraced rice paddies. It was here I formed a really close relationship with our head gardener, and he taught me not only to kite fight but also to spear fish for carp in the rice paddies. The cook, on the other hand, was my favourite. Her local dishes were amazing, although her European capabilities were limited. I've got a book of her recipes and one of my favourites is satay.'

SATAY

Ingredients

900g beef or chicken, very finely sliced
2 small red onions
2 cloves garlic
1 large fresh chilli
1 tbsp chopped fresh ginger
1 tbsp chopped galangal
1 stalk lemon grass
1 tsp coriander powder
1 tsp cumin powder
1tsp anise powder
50g castor sugar

25ml fresh lime juice
25ml tamarind water
25ml light soy sauce
1 large pinch of salt
100ml thick coconut cream

Method

1. Finely chop the onions, garlic, chilli powder, galangal and lemon grass.
2. Cut these ingredients to a fine paste in a mixer and add the coriander powder, cumin, anise powder, lime juice, tamarind water, light soy sauce and salt.
3. Add the oil, coconut cream and pour over the beef or chicken.
4. Marinate overnight. Refrigerate.

Ingredients for the sauce

8 dried red chillies
4 small red onions
3 cloves garlic
15mm knob of fresh galangal
1 stalk lemon grass
2 candlenuts
200mm stick of cinnamon
1 tsp coriander powder
1 tsp cumin powder
1 tsp turmeric
1 tsp fresh lime juice
25ml tamarind water
25g vinegar
Salt
150g roasted ground peanuts
100ml thick coconut milk
3 tbsp coconut oil

Method

1. Soak the dried chillies in cold water for about 30 minutes until soft.
2. Chop the chillies, onion, garlic, galangal, lemon grass, candlenuts and cinnamon stick and pound them together with the coriander, cumin and turmeric powders. Use a mixer for this.
3. Heat the peanut oil in a pan and stir-fry them for about 5 minutes.
4. Add the lime juice, tamarind water, sugar and salt, and continue to stir over a medium heat for a further 3 minutes.
5. Add the ground, roasted peanuts and coconut milk. Bring to the boil.
6. Lower the heat and cook until the oil rises to the surface.
7. Pour the sauce into a bowl.

For the Satay

1. Soak wooden skewers in water for about 2 hours, then thread the meat.
2. Grill to colour (dark brown).

9

BROTHERS IN ARMS

IN BANDUNG during the late 1960s the Races adopted a toddler whom they christened Jamie. About a month prior to the children flying out to join their parents for a holiday, John's stepfather had cause to head off on a feasibility study to Sirak, one of the islands in the Indonesian archipelago. In the midst of the jungle, he stumbled across an orphanage run by Dutch nuns. Dennis Race was informed that all the children had been abandoned. They were terribly sick but there was little money to purchase food or medicines, let alone for the upkeep of the ramshackle property. Looking around, he came across a child of about 14 months of age, rocking himself into a trance. The boy was on a bare mattress with no toys to play with and suffering from malnutrition. The child's mother, already having given birth to ten children, had died in childbirth. Not wanting the burden of another child, his father unceremoniously left his son under a tree. By all accounts, the father thought the child brought bad luck and hated him, because he believed the child was responsible for his wife's death.

Back at home, Dennis told Shirley about the encounter and she wanted to see the child for herself. A fortnight later, Dennis found himself back in the jungle with his wife beside him. Shirley had brought along a small teddy bear. When she slowly brought it into view, the child wet himself and suffered a febrile convulsion. The Races left the orphanage with Shirley in tears due to it having been such a traumatic and emotional experience. Once in the comfort of their hotel, she told her husband in no uncertain terms that he was to return and collect the child. Dennis obliged and, back at the orphanage for a third time, he told the nuns that he would take the child under his UN passport. Not sure whether he could legally adopt him due to officialdom, Dennis brought the toddler by plane to Jakarta and then by car to Bandung. While doctors attended to young Jamie, Dennis went through legal hoops in the adoption process. Eventually knocked back by the Indonesian government, he said he would simply pay for him. He then duly arranged for a British passport for Jamie through the British Embassy. Once in the family home, John recalls how his mother told him, Clare and Rebecca quite matter-of-factly that they had a brother.

Rebecca recalls how Jamie often fell over, having never learned to put his hands out in front of him to break his fall. As a result, it was not uncommon for him to sport lumps on his forehead. 'I remember Mum and Dad having an ex-pat party in the house in Bandung. It had this large, sweeping staircase,' she tells me. 'We were watching these drunken revellers through the bannisters. Upon being spotted by one of the guests, Jamie turned and as he ran away, tripped. As he did so, he put his hands out. It was the first time he had managed to break his fall. Mum came up the stairs to tell us off. I was crying with happiness because of what Jamie had done, and having told Mum, it was all lovely after that, although no doubt the gin helped!'

That loveliness was in short supply, sadly. John remembers how cruel his mother was to Jamie. She would often shout at him, as she had a habit of doing to all her children. To teach Jamie how to swim, Shirley literally threw him into the swimming pool in Bandung and walked away, telling her children that if they tried to save him from drowning, she would kill them. 'Terrified, all we could do was watch as he fought for his life,' John tells me.

A difficult child, Shirley dreaded the day John was first to attend school because she knew he would kick off. Rather unexpectedly, he went without a problem, and returned the same afternoon saying how much he had enjoyed it. The following morning, when she told her son it was time again to go to school, John responded, 'What do you mean, I've been to school.' According to Rebecca, from that moment, Shirley said he was a nightmare. 'Having said that, there was a particularly strong bond between our mother and John. Because he was her first born, there was always something there, and I think because of that they would squabble a lot, but then it would be all over and she would be sending him birthday presents when they were separated.' School proved particularly problematic for John. Having been diagnosed with a hearing deficiency when he was nine, the condition was a major barrier to his learning, and he would often resort to misbehaviour in class because he could not hear properly in lessons. When Shirley found out, she arranged for him to have hearing aids. With no academic leanings, John looked forward to time out of school when he could spend his pocket money on chocolate, and even resorted to taking money from his Post Office account so he could buy peaches and cream and then enjoy the spoils, hidden in the hedgerows with sister Clare.

Returning to England, John and Jamie attended Shiplake College, an independent boarding and day school by the River Thames outside Henley-on-Thames, while Rebecca joined Clare at a school in Burgess Hill, West Sussex. It was not long before Rebecca grew to hate boarding and after four terms, while her siblings continued at their respective schools, she travelled to Africa to be with her parents. During their time in England, the children enjoyed watching the science fiction television series Blake's 7. Once Rebecca relocated to Senegal, John wrote to her every week, bringing her up to date on the programme.

After Senegal, Dennis Race moved to Jakarta, Indonesia, where Rebecca would spend her school holidays. 'I think we all had a pretty good childhood, although it is trendy now to say we had a troubled one. I had some fantastic holidays because of where my mum and dad were living.' Having been schooled variously in Indonesia and Africa, Rebecca spent her last couple of years of junior school at Marycourt in Gosport, before taking O Levels at Wykeham House in the market town of Fareham.

It must have been a strange experience for the children, their parents forever travelling backwards and forwards to England due to Dennis's work schedule, leaving them at boarding school, living on occasion with their grandmother, and often being separated from each other. Rebecca, being so much younger, had a different relationship with her parents, and clearly bonded more than John or Clare ever did. They did, however, enjoy their time together and Rebecca recalls John as always having been full of high energy with, as she politely puts it, the concentration span of a gnat. Terrible to play games with, in the end his siblings refused to play with him. Cheating came naturally and he would do anything to win. If there were any sign of him losing, he would go ballistic.

Rebecca tells me that one particular Christmas when John was about 18 years old, he was sharing a bedroom with Jamie and the girls were sharing another room. It was pitch black outside. Suddenly John burst through the door and began singing When A Child Is Born. 'That is the sort of nutcase thing he would do. He was always lively. We did have a lot in common. When I was in my teens, we shared our passion for horse riding. John bought his own horse and we would ride together.'

In 1972, John was struck yet another devastating blow when he contracted hepatitis, an inflammatory condition of the liver commonly caused by a viral infection. He was desperately ill for six months. Hospitalised in Southampton, Grandma Manning and Clare would spend days and often whole nights on the floor by his bedside. With her son close to death, Shirley could not even be bothered to travel back from Thailand to spend time with her son. And yet, at odds with her total lack of affection, she always wanted her children to better themselves, and as a result was always pushing them … harder and harder. When John would come home from school and tell his mother about his day, it was never good enough. She wanted him to work hard all the time. There was little wonder that he grew up being frightened of his mother, feeling that no matter what he did, it never met her expectations. According to Rebecca, 'We were from a normal working-class family, and sometimes it went above Shirley's head. She didn't want to be reminded of her upbringing. I don't know whether John would agree with me, but I saw the other side of Mum. I think deep down he was her favourite. When she spilt from her first husband there were difficult times both emotionally and financially for her, which impacted on her children. Being the eldest child, John ended up taking a lot of the responsibility along with the flak when Mum wasn't quite with it.'

Shirley's family was poor. Her father had been a miner. As the older child, she ended up looking after two siblings; a similar situation John found himself. Having gained a place at grammar school, Shirley couldn't take it because she had to go to work instead. She was a clever, astute woman, self-taught, articulate, and well read, Rebecca tells me. 'Our parents were determined that we would all have some sort of direction. Basically, we were not allowed to simply do nothing. John was flitting around, and they told him he had to sort himself out. That resulted in a war of words between the three of them. John loved art, but I recall Mum saying once that only poofs did art. Eventually they sorted him a job in a kitchen, thinking he would hate it, and he would then have to knuckle down and do some other work, because he had been rubbish at school. Mum and Dad were thrilled to bits when John's career took off.'

John lived with Grandma Manning in his parents' house and attended St Mary's College in Bitterne Park, an eastern suburb and ward of Southampton. Private, Catholic and deeply religious, it was a rude awakening for a child who had been previously surrounded by all the privileges and material possessions afforded to a colonial household. 'I came from the school of big boys who don't cry,' he says. 'My mother was a powerhouse, and although I loved her dearly, she was a horrible woman. There was no affection, not an ounce. It was, quite frankly, horrendous. Drink and Valium, colonial extremism, parties, no morals.' His relationship with his stepfather was also nothing short of volatile. 'I remember as a teenager I had long masses of curly hair. My stepfather hated it and would threaten to cut it off. As a result, I grew up avoiding any form of violence whenever I could. If I got into a fight at school, it was only because someone had walloped me first. There are only two ways you can go.' At St Mary's College, you either fell into that pattern of bullying and violence, or you rebuffed it.

'I really believe that John felt let down by everyone when he was little,' says Clare. 'It is almost as if he has since put a barrier up between himself and the rest of the family. It is only thanks to Grandma Manning, who gave John all the motherly love that he so craved and wasn't receiving from our mother, that he has managed any level of stability in his adult life. Grandma was an amazing woman but was also very strong in character. She was what I would refer to as a nice matriarch and taught me practically everything I know. I remember being at the fairground as a teenager and some boys were flirting with me. Grandma came up, tapped me on the back of the head with her umbrella, told me to stop mixing with the ruffians and to get home immediately! She was so loving and protective, and we both adored her. Our mother, on the other hand, was awful to John. He was always trying to please her, but she almost destroyed him as a child. There is little wonder that he is so bitter.'

10

BULLETS AND BANANA CAKE

KINSHASA, FORMERLY known as Léopoldville, is the capital of the Democratic Republic of the Congo. Lying on the southern bank of the Congo River about 320 miles from the Atlantic Ocean, it is one of the largest cities of sub-Saharan Africa, and today has a population of five million. In the mid-1990s the city became the focus of the rebel uprising against the Zairian regime of Mobutu Sese Seko, who was forced out of power in 1997. The successor regime was besieged by insurgents and overburdened with newcomers, resulting in Kinshasa entering a period of severe economic hardship that persisted into the 21st century. This was not the first time there had been a crisis in the Congo. A period of political upheaval and conflict constituting a series of civil wars had occurred between 1960 and 1965, beginning almost immediately after the Congo became independent from Belgium and ended, unofficially, with the entire country being under the rule of Joseph-Désiré Mobutu. It is into this potpourri of unrest and instability that a young John Burton-Race would often spend his holidays.

After a spell in Kinshasa, Dennis and Shirley relocated to a house in Bukavu, a city in the eastern DRC, lying at the extreme southwestern edge of Lake Kivu. The children enjoyed holidays at the large family home, and John recalls his time there as just the most amazing experience. It is not surprising; today's tourists can travel the lakeside road between the towns of Gisenyi and Cyangugu, where eucalyptus trees line the route and banana trees adorn terraced hillsides. Spread out over several hills, Gisenyi is a former colonial beach resort on the northern reaches of Lake Kivu. Its former glorious past is reflected in its waterfront, lined with fading old mansions. Today, trendy bars adorn the lakeshore. The name Cyangugu refers to the two southwestern districts in Rwanda, Nyamasheke and Rusizi. The city has often been referred to as the most beautiful place in Rwanda. Here in the Congo, John would have been more used to hearing the Kinyarwanda term Abuzungu—white person or, literally, aimless wanderer. He was fortunate enough to experience wonderful safaris and would join his stepfather on feasibility trips when Dennis was covering land surveys for the construction of new roads, or on geological surveys for ore and minerals.

'I used to be out of bed by the time the sun came up and would watch amazed as the rays hit the lake. It simply sparkled,' John recalls. 'My stepfather told me, "John, I don't want to spoil it for you, but that's the sun reflecting off the millions of bullets at the bottom of the lake".' Those spent cartridges were a sad legacy from when mercenaries fought during the period of political upheaval and conflict which became known as the Congo Crisis.

With the country in constant political upheaval, it was not surprising that the children experienced plenty of unrest first-hand. There were tribes all over the area. If their parents were having a party, often going on late into the night, the houseboys would be offered somewhere to stay because they couldn't go through other tribal lands for fear of being killed. Some of the tribal men would file their teeth and one evening, one attacked Dennis in his garden. Punching to defend himself, Dennis caught his knuckle on one of the man's teeth. The knuckle became infected and Dennis became so ill that he had to go to hospital.

John, Clare, Jamie and Rebecca would go to the American Club, and on one occasion they were arrested. 'The four of us had been dropped off while

Mum and Dad went off somewhere. Soldiers came and arrested everybody in the club,' Rebecca tells me. 'On her return, Mum managed to bribe one of the soldiers to let her in, and she was then promptly arrested alongside us. Fortunately, after a lot of persuasion, we were eventually released.' Little wonder that Dennis and Shirley, when travelling as a couple, always carried first-class tickets with them, should they ever need to leave to country in a hurry whenever the soldiers had been instructed to round up civilians.

The time spent in Africa offered an enthusiastic John a world of different experiences. 'I remember meeting Amut, whose family was on the run from Idi Amin at the time of the Ugandan Bush War in the early 1980s, which was fought between the Uganda National Liberation Army and the National Resistance Army. The Indians and the Pakistanis had owned all of the retail in Uganda. His family had lost everything, so they piled what meagre possessions they had left into their Mercedes and drove to the border to escape. His parents then set up another shop in Kavu, a small town in the hills.'

The politics of the day had little effect on John's overall experience of the country, with food once again playing its part. He recalls a small café in Kinshasa where they served one of his favourite puddings, namely a slice of banana cake with a large dollop of ice cream.

BANANA CAKE

Ingredients
   250g mashed ripe bananas
   75g unsalted butter (softened)
   127g Demerara sugar
   1 vanilla pod (scrape out the seeds)
   250g plain flour
   10g baking powder
   2 large eggs
   50ml rapeseed oil
   Salt

Method

1. Mix the bananas and sugar and beat in the butter.
2. Add the dry ingredients, then the eggs, whisking all the time. Stir in the oil.
3. Bake and remove the cake after about 40 minutes. You can check when it is cooked by inserting a skewer into the cake. If it comes out clean, it is cooked.

Ingredients for Banana ice cream

1 litre milk
250g cream
300g sugar
200g egg yolks
2 ripe bananas
50ml dark rum

Method

1. Purée the bananas and stir in the rum. Place the mixture into a bowl.
2. In a pan, boil the milk and cream together and simmer.
3. In a mixing bowl, whisk the egg yolks and sugar together, add half the milk and cream, and continue to gently mix. Pour this into the remaining milk and whisk over a low heat to cook the eggs. Do not boil.
4. Remove the pan from the stove and pass the custard, whisking all the time, over the bananas. Pass the ice cream through a fine mesh sieve into a bowl to cool.
5. When cool, take the mixture to your tabletop ice cream machine to churn.

11

FAT PIG IN A TALL WHITE HAT

LEAVING HIS parents abroad, John returned to the UK to study English, History and Art A Levels at a school near Fareham, Hampshire. Three weeks in, he handed all his books back and walked out, longing to attend art college instead. But the idea met with immediate disapproval from his parents. 'Luckily, my stepfather didn't fly back from abroad and kill me. My mother then press-ganged me into cheffing, only because she was trying to teach me a lesson.' Shirley could no doubt recall when, in the Far East, John would help the family cook out. As a boy he had espied a 'huge, fat pig in a tall white hat' emerging from a restaurant kitchen and demanded of his mother what this madman did for a living. 'They hated the thought of my going to art college and remembering in the past that I had mentioned about becoming a chef, they called my bluff,' he says. 'My mother was in a rage. "I've had enough of you," she told me, "you've been a thorn in my side ever since you were born. I have fixed up five interviews for you." The first one was at this shitty hotel near Winchester. I thought, right, I'll get this bloody cow off my back. I'm going to say I want that job,' he told journalist Rachel Cooke in February 2005.

The irony would not have been lost on Shirley; it was because of her stubbornness that John's resultant passion for cooking was ignited. Despite enduring a disruptive and traumatic childhood, her son was to come out the other end having benefitted enormously from his peripatetic upbringing, absorbing the geography of the places and the markets, the smells and ingredients, carrying with him culinary influences gained from his time in Indonesia, Thailand, Dakar, Senegal and, as he says himself, 'goodness knows how many different places.' Influenced particularly by the flavours of the Far East, he went on to translate his knowledge into unique, flavoursome dishes, backed up by classic French schooling. 'I was never shy of using Far East spices, and I remember one salad I used to do with rocket and roasted skate wing with a soya vinaigrette, and it just worked.' He would steam the finely cut vegetables around the skate wings until the juices were extracted, which he would then emulsify with olive oil and soya, garlic and ginger.

Beginning an apprenticeship at The Wessex, a four-star Trust House Forte hotel in Winchester, he was thrust into a completely alien world, rubbing dirty, food-encrusted shoulders with a bag of oddballs, happily living a preternatural existence behind the kitchen doors on £9 a week. Any sane person would have turned and fled. For an immature, lonely, mentally damaged teenager, John was just too damned proud to say sorry to his teachers and re-visit the world of academia. Clare joined him as a commis chef, her foot on the very bottom rung of the ladder doing fish prep under the supervision of the section chief. After only one shift she was so tired she could barely make it back to her brother's flat. So endeth Clare's brief introduction to her brother's world.

John was dumped in the pastry section with what he called 'a madman from the Czech Republic', whose grand title was head pastry chef. He took an immediate dislike to the newbie, resulting in a particularly uncomfortable three months. He refused to answer any of John's questions, preferring to spend his time insulting him and physically kicking him up the rear. On one occasion, the kitchen team was preparing for a wedding party of 150 guests and the couple had requested a straightforward posset as one of the desserts. That job landed with John, who had no idea that a very simple dessert made in large volumes required a revised recipe. With no help from the head of section, John split the whole mixture, much to the delight of his boss, resulting in the grandest of telling offs. The mistake cost a large sum of money and it was only some months later that John's boss boasted to him that he had deliberately allowed him to make the mistake. Leaving the hotel two years later to further his career, John left the 'madman' a parting gift, something which he would not elaborate on, so one can only surmise.

LEMON POSSET WITH ELDERBERRY JELLY
(Serves 6)

Posset Ingredients
425ml double cream
125g castor sugar
2 lemons (juice only)
¼ leaf of gelatin

Method
1. Bring the cream and the soaked gelatin to the boil. Reduce the heat to a gentle simmer and cook for a further two minutes.
2. Add the lemon juice and mix thoroughly. Pass through a fine sieve and set aside to cool.
3. Skim off the foam and bubbles that surface on the top in a ladle.
4. Carefully pour the mixture into glasses and transfer them into the fridge for at least two hours to set.

Jelly Topping Ingredients
125ml elderflower cordial
75g castor sugar
274ml water
3 leaves gelatin soaked

Method

1. Soak the gelatin leaves in half of the water, place half the cordial and the other half of the water in a pan with the sugar and bring to the boil.
2. Take off the heat and add the gelatin. Once dissolved, add the rest of the water and the cordial. Pour into a bowl to cool.
3. When cold, top the lemon possets and return to the fridge to set.

A fascination with his workmates and working environment proved pivotal for John, and he quickly found favour with a troubleshooting chef named Eugene Basini, who took the youngster under his wing. Basini immediately recognised management potential in the young man but John would have none of it. Basini instead put him forward for a number of cookery competitions, and his victories eventually paved the way for a transfer to Quaglino's, at Hotel Meurice in Bury Street, in the St James's district of London. A former haven for Hollywood legends and the political elite, an impressionable John Burton-Race had suddenly gatecrashed a surreal world of elitist dining, the order of the day being the preparation of classic dishes from both sides of the Channel.

Attending Highbury College one day a week with workmate Derek Baker, John lived on the top floor of a mansion block at the back of Shepherd's Bush Green, near White City. Though earning an increased salary of £11.50 a week, he could not afford to feed the meter and so the flat would be freezing in winter, with ice often forming on the inside of the windows. He slept fully clothed, underneath a dressing gown and bedding for extra warmth. Not terribly hygienic, admittedly, but it provided a modicum of comfort. The school of hard knocks continued for John through his first month, when his locker was broken into and his wages stolen. The second month, his room was broken into and most of his clothes and other belongings were taken.

Working anything from 10 to 12 hours a day on either early or late shifts, six days a week, there was little social life to enjoy. Any down time was spent sinking a few pints, eating kebabs and playing poker. It was all to prove a steep learning curve. Pranks were par for the course during a day's graft. On one occasion, John and his fellow preppers got together with the lads on the pastry section with the idea of picking out all the seeds from their Marijuana stash, floating them in a handful of greenery and making up a selection of Madeira cakes in readiness for afternoon tea. Despite some of the resin seeping out of the mixture, the cakes went down a storm. Oh, how those jolly old ladies must have skipped down the street, handbags swinging as they made their merry way home. The joke, however, backfired on some members of the kitchen team, who were duly dismissed. John managed to slip through the net. Never into drugs like some of his workmates, he avoided eating any of the cake.

Beavering away in the small hotel, John lapped up the daily challenges as diners flocked to the restaurant to enjoy all types of seasonal game dishes, offering John the opportunity to cook and eat grouse for the first time in his life. Today, grouse remains one of his favourite game dishes.

ROAST GROUSE
(Serves 4)

Ingredients
4 young grouse
1½ litres brown chicken stock
2 tbsp red wine vinegar
1 tbsp redcurrant jelly
½ litre red wine
1 glass ruby port
4 juniper berries (crushed)
1 sprig thyme
1 bay leaf
1 onion
1 carrot
4 shallots
1 leek
1 stick celery
4 cloves garlic

Salt

Pepper

30g butter

30g oil

20g chopped liver

Method

1. Take all the grouse and remove the breastbones. Season with salt and pepper. Remove the livers.

2. Heat a large roasting tray and add a little oil. Sear the grouse to a golden brown colour.

3. Roast in a medium oven for about 11 minutes. Remove from the pan to rest.

4. To bone the grouse, take off the legs in one piece and remove the breasts. Bone out the thighbone and clean around the drumstick, pulling out any darkened part, which has been near the chest cavity, as this can be bitter and unpleasant.

5. Keep the prepared grouse on a buttered tray covered with buttered greaseproof paper. Chop up the carcasses. In the same roasting pan, add a small amount of butter, the bones and the chopped vegetables. Remove them when brown with a slotted spoon to a bowl. Tip out the excess and de-glaze the pan with red wine vinegar.

6. Boil rapidly, scraping off any sediment. Add the redcurrant jelly and crushed juniper berries. When sticky, put back the bones and vegetables, stirring all the time. When glazed, remove the bones and vegetables to a large saucepan. Add the red wine, boil and reduce to liquid by half of its volume.

7. Pour in a large glass of port. Boil and add the brown chicken stock. Add the garlic, thyme and bay leaf. Bring back to the boil. Remove all the surfacing impurities with a ladle and discard.

8. Turn down the sauce to a simmer and cook for about 15 minutes.

9. Strain the sauce through a fine mesh sieve into another pan and reduce the sauce by half of its original volume.

10. As the sauce is nearing completion, re-heat the grouse. Pass the sauce through a muslin cloth to trap all the blood particles. Bring the sauce back to a gentle boil and at the last minute, off the boil, whisk in the butter and chopped liver.

Enjoy together with game chips, baby Brussels sprouts, celeriac purée and sugar-glazed blackberries. Finish with a base of wilted watercress and if at all practical, top the grouse with a slice of sautéed Foie Gras.

12

LOONY TUNES

THE HEAD chef at Quaglino's was a German by the name of Karl Hermann Wadsack. 'A total lunatic, but I loved him to bits,' recalls John. 'He would do some of the most extraordinary things for which he would be locked up for today for being a racist. He would, for example, get the kitchen staff to be heads of Panzer Divisions and play war games.' When Wadsack moved to the internationally famous Chewton Glen Hotel, in Hampshire, as Chef de Cuisine he took John and another chef, Stephen Treadwell, with him. On arrival, the 6ft 5in tall Wadsack, with the personality of someone 8ft tall, called the existing staff together for an introductory meeting. Flanked by John to his right and Stephen to his left and in his heavy German accent, he asked the assembled team, 'Do you want the good news or the bad news?' At first no one answered, so he simply repeated the question. One of the chefs then replied, 'The good news,' to which Wadsack responded, 'The good news is that I am here with my boys.' Nervous laughter filled the room. The same chef then asked, 'And the bad news, chef?' 'Oh, that's easy,' replied Wadsack. 'The bad news is that you are all fucked.' He then fired the entire kitchen and front-of-house staff. Owner Martin Scanlon went mental but, true to form, Wadsack spun round and told him that if he did not get out of his kitchen, he would be 'floured'. So, there they were, Wadsack, John Burton-Race and Stephen Treadwell, the three Musketeers.

Every Sunday lunch at Chewton Glen was a manic experience. Chef kept a very small a la carte menu on, and although 80 per cent of the offering was a set menu at a set price, the most popular choice was roast beef and according to John, this was no ordinary roast beef. The secret to its taste was that the beef was cooked with rendered beef marrow, also used in the making of the red wine sauce.

ROAST BEEF
(serves 8)

Beef Marrow Fat Ingredients
12 split marrowbones
1 whole head of garlic
1 bunch chives

Method
1. Lay out the marrowbones in a roasting tray. Cut the garlic head in two. Sprinkle the thyme over the bones and place in the oven on a low heat (120°F) to melt the marrow and fats. Do this the night before. It takes about 4 hours.
2. Remove the tray and carefully scrape out any marrow that has not melted. With a scraper, push it through a fine mesh sieve into a bowl. Discard the bones and strain the fats over the marrow. Reserve aside.

Sauce Ingredients
2 tbsp marrow fat
500g beef trimmings
6 shallots (finely sliced)

2 cloves garlic

1 sprig thyme

6 medium mushrooms (sliced)

1 glass Ruby port

½ bottle red wine

600ml veal stock (if not available, 600ml brown chicken stock)

Method

1. Heat the marrow fat in a large saucepan. Add the beef trimmings and cook until brown.
2. Add the sliced shallots and cook to a golden colour. Add the garlic, thyme and sliced mushrooms.
3. Pour in the port and reduce until it becomes sticky.
4. Add the red wine and boil to reduce by half.
5. Add the veal stock. Bring the sauce to the boil and with a ladle, take off the surfacing fat and impurities. Discard them.
6. Turn the sauce down to a simmer and cook for a further hour.
7. Strain the sauce and reduce the liquid until the required flavour and consistency has been achieved.

Chewton Glen Hotel always used a sirloin on the bone. This recipe will work for a filet or a strip loin. Use the remaining rendered beef and marrow fat to make the Yorkshire puddings.

With service at Chewton Glen resumed, John would spend his time in the larder at the back of the kitchen, out of harm's way … or so he thought. If he were late with a starter, Wadsack would call out his name, swear and tell him to get a move on. Thirty seconds later, the instruction would be repeated. One particular Saturday evening, Wadsack called out John's name. As he peered cautiously around the corner of the larder door, one of chef's large white clogs came flying through the air and struck him plumb on the temple. John crumpled to the floor, out for the count. A fretting Stephen Treadwell, John's colleague in the larder, eventually managed to rouse him. Conscious that his fledgling career had been possibly catapulted into a vat of blancmange, John raised his head cautiously, blood dripping down his temple and into his eye. The goliath Wadsack towered over him and, never one to mince his words and without an ounce of sympathy, inquired, 'Are you going to serve fucking table 17 or not?'

John recalls the veg chef having massive sideburns and so was nicknamed Biggles by his workmates, after the famous aviator. Biggles drove a Lotus Europa, which Wadsack was happy to refer to as 'a piece of English plastic shit'. The big man drove a BMW 2002 Turbo. Often drunk during service, he would rant at anyone who dared cross his path — staff or customer, no matter. Tired of having his beloved car slagged off, Biggles, normally a man of few words, challenged chef to a race after service had ended. The staff held their breath, expecting Wadsack to bury Biggles in the driveway's Tarmac for his impudence. Instead, he took the bait. The finish line was the Sandpiper Inn, in the village of Mudeford, the forfeit to the loser being to buy everyone a drink. Along the drive, over the speed humps, the two cars headed nose to tail out of the car park and onwards to New Milton, along the main road on the edge of the New Forest. Intent on taking a shortcut to Mudeford, Wadsack overshot a sharp right-hander, broadsided a telephone box, wrote his car off and landed up in hospital. Two weeks later he returned to work, stitched up and swathed in bandages, and without his driving licence, taken off him on a charge of drink-driving. He called Biggles over and claimed it had not been a proper race, to which an affronted Biggles replied, 'I won, and you owe me a beer.' Not a smart move, as Wadsack promptly sacked him.

It fell on John to give the car-less Wadsack a lift to work. On one occasion, chef took his wife's car. When Chewton Glen reception said she had been calling the restaurant, he claimed it could not have been his wife as he had locked her in the bathroom, and there she could stay all day as far as he was concerned. He had clearly forgotten about the window, through which she had made her escape.

With a reputation to match his size, Karl Wadsack went on to be awarded an illustrious two stars at Chewton Glen. His son, Joe, a respected chef, wine expert and television celebrity in his own right, gained his love of food from his larger-than-life father, who was Egon Ronay's Chef of the Year in 1976. After Chewton Glen, Karl and his wife operated a highly successful gastro pub, winning Egon Ronay's Pub of the Year award. While his brother was upstairs watching Family Fortunes, Joe found it more exciting to watch his father steaming around the kitchen swearing. He was in awe, wondering how a man in advancing years was able to deliver perfection to 90 people almost every night virtually on his own. Joe accredits much of his skill in the kitchen to the punishments his father used to give him. Scraping mussels, picking parsley and thyme, grating endless blocks of Parmesan ... it was all worth it in the end.

13

BOHEMIAN RHAPSODY

WILD, SINGLE-MINDED and single-tracked, you might understandably presume that John Burton-Race has breezed through life with reckless abandon, in harness with a sense of purpose and vigour, forever wanting to be the best he can be. Always one to speak his mind no matter the situation, whether good or bad, he will often see things from a different angle, or simply his way. For some, he probably does not make sense. Should he find himself in a sociable situation where he feels uncomfortable, there are two ways to go: you can power down and be really quiet and keep yourself to yourself, or you can do what he normally does, and that is to drink copious amounts of wine and become objectionably rude and loud, which then pisses people off even more. In a nutshell, he finds sanctuary behind the doors of the kitchen, because he has had to endure so many disappointments on the outside, particularly when he was growing up. Even as a young man, he would throw himself wholeheartedly into a situation, such as with his first marriage to Marie-Christine Bordeau. At that time, he did not realise he was not in love, but he knew he was lonely. As a result, he ended up grabbing on to someone who in turn grabbed on to him. It is almost as if he likes to move in safe investment areas. Perhaps he and Marie-Christine were both looking for something that was not there in the first place. For John's part, it would appear he was looking for the emotional attachment and family security that bypassed him throughout his childhood. For John, that first foray into wedlock felt right at the time.

His talent and enormous ambition saw him in France with Marie-Christine, whose family was already well established in the hotel and catering industry. They knew the culture of cooking and the importance of food and wine. Catering for those looking for the contemporary, it was all very avant-garde. For someone totally allergic to the normal work ethic, John suddenly found himself mainlining on an established world of true originality and entrepreneurship. The courting couple would drive around France visiting different locations and restaurants, savouring classic French cuisine as they went. The white, middle-class bohemian, this new-kid-on-the-block upstart who had been happy to skirt the edge of the establishment during his training in London found himself playing by someone else's rules. Oddly, his first instinct was to kick out against the opportunity his new family was offering him on a plate. Possibly, he objected to being thrust into the limelight. It was not to last, as over time John formed a special affinity with his future father-in-law.

14

FRENCH DRESSING

HAVING GRAFTED his way through the lowly ranks of kitchen life, learning and honing his craft as he moved from one establishment to the next, in the late 1970s John found himself working under the wing of the French Michelin-starred chef Raymond Blanc at Les Quat'Saisons in Summertown, Oxfordshire. 'Before I came across John, I came across his mother, which was a more frightening sight!' Blanc tells me. 'I remember her being small and tough, and she was wearing a red dress. She said to me, "You be good to my son." My God, it put fear in my eyes. As for John, I felt he was a person who was totally driven; a person who loved what he was doing; a professional. I could sense he was committed to excellence with no compromise, and at that time I was looking for SAS-type troopers who would achieve what I wanted to achieve. He started as a young chef de partie and he was a pillar, with all the qualities of a hard-working man and very well skilled. I had never cooked under a chef and he knew more than I did, because I had been self-taught, so I learned certain techniques from him, but equally he learned a lot from me.'

John recalls arriving at Les Quat'Saisons and quickly realising that Raymond Blanc knew little about the basics of cookery. 'I turned up having worked a classic background in one-star Michelin hotels, and there was this little guy who was madder than me, barking mad in fact, but he clearly made up for any lack of culinary knowledge with total enthusiasm. I remember he would read and read and had this wonderful saying—"Go on and get on with it".' John must have wondered exactly what he had let himself in for. At Les Quat'Saisons, while Blanc's vision for his food was fine, the working environment was something else entirely, with the small team beavering away in a kitchen with no insulation. In the winter it was minus two degrees and in the summer 50-plus. 'It was an extraordinarily tough working environment, 2.5 metres by four metres, and behind the kitchen was all the storage in a corrugated iron tub measuring six metres by 1.5 metres,' says Blanc. 'We were working during the worst possible time England had known for years due to a recession and later the miners' strikes. The culture of Le Manoir, however, was born in that tiny place, where people mattered, guests mattered, my team mattered and excellence mattered, and we would never settle for anything less than excellence. There were rows with my then wife Jenny, who wanted to make more money, and to me it was just selling out. It is never easy.'

The 40-seater former Greek restaurant was hidden away in a 1960s concrete parade of shops, squeezed in between a lingerie shop and Oxfam's Oxfordshire headquarters. Despite its location, it quickly proved popular with diners. Initially, John worked in this desperately cramped, hot, sweaty environment—a tiny working area was as small as your average domestic kitchen and built as a lean-to—shoulder to shoulder with four other cooks in a Michelin establishment. Blanc nicknamed John the British Bulldog. Anything he found too taxing or when he felt the need to sack someone, he leaned on John to do the dirty work. In the cash-strapped world of John Burton-Race, never the greatest strategist when it came to diplomacy in the kitchen, he was happy to oblige. They must have been like two peas in a pod, each oozing talent and raw ambition. As part of the onward advance of cooking entrepreneurship, Blanc saw something special in John and was ever eager to support his originality and creative energy.

John found himself working alongside the notorious Nigel Marriage, and from the outset theirs was a fiery relationship; the young, headstrong, aspiring Marriage confiding in Fiona Sims in an interview for the Caterer and Hotelkeeper: 'There was a bit of a fracas between us but it was good after that. Now we're like brothers.'

To Blanc, Nigel Marriage was a good man, but he was too much like John. 'I had two hyper chefs in a tiny kitchen,' he says. 'John and Nigel were crazy. There was a degree of animosity and bad behaviour between them. They would go outside, and they would fight. Both were good on their own. I think Nigel was even crazier than he was. As a boss it is frightening, because if you stand to lose two of your senior people it is difficult, and at the time I did not know how to handle the situation between them, because they were very strong-willed.'

Around this time, chefs were generally perceived as a lowly bunch, and this created an industry that had no particular structure. It was lawless, where violence was rife. Blanc is quick to point out that he personally never 'put my fist on anyone or threatened anyone'.

'I have shouted, oh yes, but it was always about excellence. It was never, ever personal. A lot of people made it personal, and I knew very quickly that it was wrong. I am one of the lucky ones, because I saw around me so much violence growing up, and I did not want to create an industry like that. A bit of boisterous behaviour is fine.' Blanc is conscious that part of the image problem of the catering industry today is that it self-harmed for so long. 'Who wants to work 12 or 15 hours a day? Who wants to be beaten up or sworn at, to be degraded in front of everyone?' he tells me. 'Nobody wants to work on Christmas Day or over New Year, or if they do, they want to be treated decently. If today's chefs acted like they did in the past, they would be in jail today. It is over. We are now entertaining a new and exciting world. I always wanted to create such a world, but it was never easy, because you had so many hotheaded people around you. I always wanted to create a modern industry where you as a papa would be happy to send your child, who in turn would be happy in the kitchen, knowing that your child was going to be well looked after, trained and supported. People never learn through abject cruelty. And we have seen so much of it on television of chefs humiliating and bullying others.'

Hotheaded he may well have been but in Blanc's kitchen, John remained totally focused on his work and remained respectful to his boss. Within a matter of months, Blanc saw in him qualities that were rare, including an obsession with perfection, similar to himself. 'He was helping me realise my dream, which was total excellence and no compromise. At the time I did not know how to compromise. You learn to do that as you grow older because if you don't, you die. For many chefs, it is difficult to know how to reconciliate business with ideals. It took me years to understand there is an acceptable middle ground, and it is not selling out, but when you are creating food you need a proper margin, not creating dishes for £7 and selling them for £10. I had to learn how to make money, because I did not know how, as I had never been taught. It is so crucial. My then wife was looking after the finances, but it was me in the kitchen and I was in this bubble, so I had a big problem at first and it took me a long time to adjust. I had lots of arguments with her."

Prior to joining Blanc's establishment, Nigel Marriage spent four years as head chef at Michael's Nook Country House, in Grasmere, Cumbria. Reg Gifford had purchased the Victorian building in 1967. At that time, the entrepreneur also owned an antiques business and a restaurant in the village called Two Singing Birds, which closed in the early 1980s. Initially using the property as his home, he re-opened it as a country house hotel and restaurant in 1969, and it gained a Michelin star. The hotel ceased trading in 2002.

Marriage's career was spawned after attending Portsmouth Catering College, followed by a position at the Savoy. 'Trompetto was the man in charge in those days. He was a hard man. He used to walk around with an apron rolled up like a truncheon under his arm—put the fear of God into you,' he told Fiona Sims. Marriage also spent time at Dartmouth's Carved Angel under renowned chef Joyce Molyneux. John was to take over the restaurant later in his career, re-branding it as The New Angel.

The Savoy had appointed Silvino Stefano Trompetto as its first British head chef in 1965, a position he retained until 1980. Notoriously sexist, Trompetto held the belief that no woman should ever be allowed to work in his kitchens, not even in the pastry department. In 1975, he was taken to task by restaurateur, chef and television presenter Prue Leith. She approached Trompetto and to take on a young female graduate of Leith's School of Food and Wine on a two-week trial. Expecting a retort about girls taking men's minds off the job, his refusal and resultant explanation left her flabbergasted. 'Because, dear lady,' the chef boomed, 'at a certain time of the month, women cause the mayonnaise to curdle,' adding for good measure, 'that is why women are not allowed into the mushroom sheds in France. They stop the spores germinating.' Trompetto went on to receive an MBE from the Queen in 1974. The irony might not have been lost on Trompetto in later years, as plaudits began to rain down on female chefs. For example, in 2018 Clare Smyth, the owner of Core in London's Notting Hill, was named Best Female Chef in the World. Clare was, in fact, the first woman to hold three Michelin stars in the UK, when she was head chef at Restaurant Gordon Ramsay. She joined an illustrious list, including Angela Hartnett and Sally Clarke. Hark even further back to the ground-breaking French chef Eugénie Brazier. Born in La Tranclière, she opened her first restaurant, La Mère Brazier, in 1921, turning the small grocery store into a high-end establishment. According to the food blog Eater, 'on opening day, she served lunch and dinner, crayfish with mayonnaise and pigeon with peas. It was a simple and elegant space; the main room had large bay windows overlooking the street and earthenware tiles on the walls in cream, grey and blue.' The mother of French cooking went on to revolutionise the culinary world. Accorded three Michelin stars in 1933, Brazier repeated the feat with her second restaurant, Col de la Luere, in the foothills of the Alps. It was a record that stayed with her until 1998, when the French-born chef Alain Ducasse was awarded his second set of three stars.

15

CULINARY HERO

RAYMOND BLANC was born in Besançon in the Franche-Comté region of eastern France in 1949. While his two sisters learned their cookery skills under Maman Blanc, he was taught the art of foraging by their father in the kitchen garden. Having originally trained as a waiter, in 1972 Blanc was fired after taking the unwise decision of offering the head chef advice on how to cook. The manager dispatched him across the English Channel to The Rose Revived in Newbridge, Oxfordshire, where he later married Jenny, the owner's daughter.

By September 1977, a couple of months before his 28th birthday, Blanc had amassed three months of restaurant experience under the tutelage of chef-patron André Chavagnon, who had opened the French restaurant La Sorbonne, in Oxford, in 1966. The multi award-winning chef's restaurant appeared regularly in the Michelin Guide through the 1960s and 1970s, and its many celebrity diners included Sir Paul McCartney and Princess Diana. Chavagnon, who passed away in his hometown of Roanne, France, in 2017, also trained fellow French chef Michel Sadones, who became well known on the Oxford catering scene. For an impatient Blanc, those three months were enough. Riding on a wave of energy and optimism rather than solid business acumen he and Jenny opened Les Quat'Saisons in Summertown, on the wrong side of the tracks as far as Oxford was concerned. Within two years, however, it was awarded its first Michelin star and named Egon Ronay Guide Restaurant of the Year. With his career on a constantly upward trajectory, Blanc focused on a bigger culinary prize and in 1981 opened La Maison Blanc, a chain of boulangeries and patisseries that also contained cafés. In January 1982, Les Quat'Saisons received its second Michelin star. In the same year, Blanc took a bolder step up the culinary ladder when he acquired a particularly attractive manor house in the Oxfordshire village of Great Milton, with the help of a government grant and investment from friends and regulars from Les Quat'Saisons in return for a stake. In 1984 he opened Le Manoir Aux Quat'Saisons as a country house hotel and the restaurant soon achieved double Michelin starred status.

To gain experience either working in restaurants in France or having the opportunity to hone one's craft under a Frenchman's tutelage in England was on every aspiring chef's wish list, with classic French cuisine topping the menu. However, the opportunity to learn such skills was not as accessible then as it is today and there were fewer chefs in Europe at the time. Scandinavia didn't have its Michelin guide, America didn't have any Michelin stars, Spain was in its infancy and although the Michelin guide was branching out, France was the dominant factor when it came to cuisine and, as a result, French chefs were looked upon as the innovative force. The likes of the Roux brothers, Pierre Koffman and Raymond Blanc were all playing to the tune of the classics and French cuisine. Les Quat'Saisons mirrored the style but Blanc made it somehow lighter, while television both defined and added to it with a freedom that chefs have enjoyed ever since. Today's young chefs can travel to America, Spain, France, Scandinavia, or indeed stay on home turf and work their way through Michelin-starred restaurants, sound in the acknowledge that the generation before them had carved out the route many cooks now follow, gaining their skills in the style of classic French cuisine.

In conversation with renowned British chef Michael Caines, he tells me there was nothing classic about the way Blanc applied his craft. 'He was light and open-minded, and he changed the way when the zenith was very classical. What you get from the classics is a base of technical knowledge. In the 1980s and 1990s, there were nine two-star and three three-stars, and certainly not that many one-star restaurants. That is not to say Michelin stars were harder to get then, but there was simply not the abundance of skill. What happened was we tended to find that the top restaurants in the UK were a bundle of excellence, whereas now we have been thinned out. John Burton-Race helped pave the way by advancing his knowledge and giving the opportunity for others to work in the kitchen and go on in their own right. His contribution to that culinary process and achievement was massive, and he was definitely up there with the best of them.'

Without doubt, the culinary bus has forever been a hard one to stay on and enjoying the pace is clearly punishing work, but in those days, chefs such as John Burton-Race, Marco Pierre White and Martin Blunos were busy defining the future of the culinary map of Britain. They were responsible for making the next generation realise they didn't have to be French or travel to France when the landscape around them was changing so rapidly.

Michel Roux Senior tells me how important it is to recognise the importance of classic cuisine as it was and still is, because that remains the basis of knowledge of haute cuisine. Once a chef understands how to cook something properly, to take it and adapt it and move it forward, there is not a lot that has gone on since those early days that has made that much of an impact in cooking. Ultimately, while new techniques have become reliant on classic techniques, they are done in a modern, contemporary way, and in this respect not all that is done in the kitchen is a million miles away from what was done 30 years ago.

For John, even today Raymond Blanc remains one of his culinary heroes. 'I love his style of cooking,' he tells me. 'As for a recipe, there are hundreds, but one that I always enjoyed is the way he uses veal kidneys. I love this dish with wilted spinach or watercress. Serve it with potato purée cooked in skins with a little hot milk, butter and truffle oil.' This is John's spin on a Blanc staple.

VEAL KIDNEYS, SHALLOT PUREE
AND RED WINE SAUCE
(Serves 4)

Ingredients

2 veal kidneys in their fat
1 tbsp oil
Salt and ground pepper
Shallot Purée Ingredients
8 shallots or 2 white onions (sliced)
2 cloves garlic (peeled)
80g unsalted butter
½ lemon (the juice of)
1 dessertspoon castor sugar
1 sprig thyme

Method

1. In a saucepan melt the butter over a medium heat and add the
   shallots. Add the garlic and gently cook in the butter, no colour.
2. Add the lemon juice, sugar, a little salt and milled white pepper.
   Add the thyme and a cup of water or light chicken stock.
3. Put a lid on the pan and cook in the oven for about 30 minutes
   with the oven at 180°C.
4. When cooked, remove the pan from the oven. Discard the thyme
   and scrape out all the shallots into the mixture. Purée until smooth.
   Put the shallot purée into a little pan with a knob of cold butter on
   top. Place a lid on and reserve aside.

Sauce Ingredients

4 shallots (peeled and sliced)
40g unsalted butter
1 clove garlic (peeled and crushed)
½ bay leaf

1 sprig thyme

1 sprig fresh tarragon

½ glass port

1 glass red wine

150ml veal stock or brown chicken stock

2 tbsp cream

1 tsp Dijon mustard

Method

1. In a saucepan, over a medium heat, melt the butter and quickly add the shallots. Add the garlic, ½ bay leaf, thyme and tarragon. Cook without colour for about 5 minutes or until tender. Add the port and cook until the liquid is reduced and becomes sticky.

2. Add the red wine, boil and reduce until it has virtually gone.

3. Pour in the veal/chicken stock. Bring the pan to the boil. Skim off the surfacing impurities with a ladle and discard.

4. Turn the sauce down to a brisk simmer and reduce the liquid by half. Pass the sauce through a fine mesh strainer into another pan. Bring the liquid back to the boil and add the cream. Once thickened, take the pan off the heat and whisk into the mustard. Check the seasoning, and add a little salt, pepper and lemon juice to taste. Reserve aside.

Cooking the kidneys

1. Trim the excess fat from the kidneys, leaving a thin layer all the way round.

2. Cut the kidneys lengthways into two and carefully cut sinews exposed in the middle. Season with salt and lots of black, milled pepper.

3. Preheat the oven to 200°C. On the stove place a sauté pan and heat it.

4. When the pan is hot, add a little oil. Place in the kidneys and sear them golden brown.

5. Put the kidneys in the oven and roast them for about 15 minutes.

6. When cooked, remove the pan and place the kidneys on a tray to rest. As the kidneys rest, they will give out some juices and blood. Strain these into the prepared sauce.

Serving

1. Warm the kidneys in the oven for a few minutes.
2. Heat the shallot purée and spoon a tablespoon down the middle of your serving plate.
3. Reheat the sauce, but do not boil it.
4. Remove the kidneys from the oven. With a very sharp knife, finely slice them and lay the slices down on top of the purée.
5. Spoon a little sauce over the top of the kidney slices and a little more around.

16

REVOLUTIONARY GUARD

I N 1984, Blanc moved to the 15th century manor in Great Milton and opened Le Manoir aux Quat'Saisons as a restaurant with rooms. The cookery school, L'Ecole de Cuisine, opened in 1991, and the following year he teamed up with Virgin Hotels to expand the property with 32 bedrooms. Virgin bailed in 2002.

While Blanc's eye was on excellence at Le Manoir, he was also attracted to the idea of opening a brasserie, somewhere he could create hearty dishes. After five years of grafting at Les Quat'Saisons, he took the bold step of re-branding as Le Petit Blanc in the original Summertown premises, appointing John as head chef.

Blanc's aim had always been to make the French philosophy of good food central to good living in the UK by creating and serving food to be enjoyed by the masses, from the time-conscious person to those looking for a welcoming family restaurant. The idea of rolling out affordable, quality food was pivotal to his success, food very much defined by Maman Blanc's influences. No doubt he was also enamoured by the esoteric mix of artists, writers and philosophers that were drawn to eat, drink and engage in small talk at such establishments, something he had previously witnessed in France.

It was to be a different philosophy at Le Manoir. His vision came at a time of revolution in fine dining, with a certain sector of the public desirous of eating exceptional food in bespoke settings where they could experience luxury on a plate, paying extraordinary prices for food that they perceived as being extraordinarily special. Like magpies, the wealthy soon flocked to a growing eclectic mix of aesthetically pleasing establishments where chefs, already skirting the shadowlands of celebrity status, were happy to cater for diners with deep pockets. The main driving force for this food revolution was London, where the chic aesthetic had percolated into every nook and cranny of architecture, which lent itself to a designer-led restaurant setting. Alongside established chefs, young upstarts — the likes of Marco Pierre White, John Burton-Race and Alistair Little — later became a part of the vanguard of the revolution, preparing England's cities as driving forces in the world of gastronomy.

John had introduced his brother Jamie to Blanc. In a rut and with no career path in mind, Jamie signed up for a three-year apprenticeship scheme at Le Manoir, albeit somewhat reluctantly. The brothers were not destined to work together as John had already accepted the head chef's position at Le Petit Blanc, telling him, 'It wouldn't be a good environment for you to work with me because you need to learn the hard way, on your own.'

Le Petit Blanc was packed with diners every day and while the food was quite simple, it was also classically French. One of the most popular dishes was the herb-crusted lamb. It sold so well, in fact, that it rather put John off lamb for quite a long while!

HERB-CRUSTED LAMB
(Serves 4)

Ingredients
2 racks of new season lamb (French trimmed)
2 tbsp olive oil
1 tbsp Dijon mustard

Salt

Pepper

Ingredients for the Herb Crust

Large bunch of flat leaf parsley (picked and finely chopped)

2 sprigs of fresh thyme (leaves picked from the stalk and finely chopped)

4 cloves garlic (crushed and finely chopped)

150g breadcrumbs

1 tbsp olive oil

Method

1. In a food processor add the parsley, thyme, garlic and rosemary. Chop to a purée.

2. Add the breadcrumbs and carefully pulse the mixture a little at a time until the breadcrumbs are mixed with the herbs. Be careful not to over-mix the crumb or it will form a horrible ball.

3. Lastly, pulse in the olive oil for 2 or 3 seconds. Pour the crumb out on to a tray.

To Cover and Cook the Lamb

1. Pre-heat the oven to 200°C.

2. In a large frying pan heat the olive oil. Score the fat of the lamb racks and season with salt and lots of black pepper.

3. When the oil is hot, lay down the racks of lamb and sear the meat. Turn the racks on their sides and sear them all over golden brown for 5 minutes.

4. When seared, put the pan in the oven to roast for about 5 minutes. Remove the lamb to rest for 5 minutes.

5. With a pastry brush, brush the Dijon mustard all over the lamb.

6. When covered with mustard, press them down into the herb crumb, making sure it is completely covered, except for the bones.

7. Put the herb-crusted lamb back into the frying pan and place in the oven to cook for about 8 minutes.

Serve with a little lamb jus. Gratin Dauphinoise potatoes and tomato fondue works with this dish.

Work at Le Petit Blanc and Le Manoir was hectic but there was still time for the occasional late evening wind-down with friends. One particular evening, Raymond Blanc, Marco Pierre White, John and another friend met for drinks at the Springs Spa Hotel and Golf Club in Wallingford. Drinks turned to more drinks, and eventually they were all as drunk as skunks, so what did they do … they decided to have a horse race. John, on all fours, was one of the two horses, with Blanc as his jockey. Marco was the other horse. Once his jockey mounted, off they went hell for leather across the dining room. John and Blanc lost by two races to one, and that was only because at one point during the last race Marco kicked John's arm from under him and as a result, Blanc went flying into a table, sending it and its contents crashing to the ground. (John would neither confirm nor deny that Raymond had, in fact, been carrying a whip and was riding naked at the time!). After having been asked to leave the establishment on several occasions, eventually they stumbled out at about 2.15am. Several days later, Blanc received a letter from the general manager of the hotel, stating under no uncertain terms that not only was he and his cronies banned for life, but also anyone associated with either Le Manoir or Le Petit Blanc.

Blanc's vision for Le Petit Blanc had been to create what Great Britain needed the most at that time: a small bistro serving top-quality, but affordable food, which was both fresh and seasonal. It harked back to his childhood and everything his mother taught him. 'I chose John as head chef because he knew my food,' Blanc tells me. 'I knew also that he was able, and his enthusiasm was so contagious. I gave him a brief because he was a good man and I trusted him completely. I also knew people would follow him there. I wanted affordable food at Petit Blanc. I said what I wanted was a bistro. Lovely little recipes, beautifully formed, but not expensive because that was what was missing so badly in the UK. The problem then was that while John knew my food, he couldn't disassociate himself from the food I was doing at Les Quat'Saisons, which was not what I wanted to do at Petit Blanc.'

Writing in his autobiography, A Taste Of My Life, Blanc noted: 'He (John) did so well that the "brasserie"' got a Michelin star in his first year. Great achievement, maybe, but I wanted a star as much as a hole in the head: now it was competing with Le Manoir. It did not make any sense.' As far as Blanc was concerned, in his 18 months at Petit Blanc, John had undermined everything he was trying to achieve. While it was indeed a beautiful place, John was creating too high a standard of food that did not fit with the original brief and Blanc, as owner, found himself in danger of competing against himself. 'I was shooting myself in the foot, and he had to go. I could see what was happening, but I was not strong enough as a businessman to take command straight away, because I was still learning myself. While the opportunity had been wonderful for John, it had proved to be unfortunate for me, in that he was not working for me anymore, he was working for himself, his status and his name. He was working on his brand on my back. Even if he didn't know it, that is what he was doing. We had conversations about it. He could have cooked another way, but that is what he had decided to do. His actions undermined everything I was trying to achieve, although I don't think John ever did it in a malicious way. Then I sold because the damage was done.' Bruno Loubet had taken over the brasserie from John and ran it for two years, during which time he crystallised the concept. While it was by this time a luxurious conservatory, as far as Blanc was concerned it did not fit the surroundings. 'As we all know, John and Bruno went on to achieve great things for themselves,' he noted.

According to Gary Jones, today the Executive Head Chef at Le Manoir, it had never been Blanc's intention to gain another Michelin star. 'John always put a lot of work and effort in and as a result has always produced great food,' he tells me. Unfortunately for John, such excellence proved to be his undoing at Petit Blanc.

Jones joined the Blanc stable in 1999, bringing with him the disciplines and techniques of classic French cuisine expected from someone who had worked at both the Waterside Inn and Waldo's at Cliveden. Jones, from Merseyside, applied himself early to his chosen career, aiming to become a world-class chef. His mother had an influence on him. 'She was a great cook,' he tells me. 'She ended up cooking for kids in an orphanage after she was shipped off to the Lakes. She then became a nanny, cooking for a family. I used to find these Mediterranean cookbooks when I was 10 years old and enjoyed looking at the colours in the pictures. Mum always did a great spread. I realised then how great food can turn people from being miserable into having a great time by making them happy. I remember when I was 12, Mum did the catering for a wedding in the village hall. I was doing the washing up but got a great buzz from helping her create the menu. She would holiday in Paris and bring back menus. All of these things had an influence on me.'

Jones completed a two-year catering course at Carlett Park on the Wirral, picking up kitchen knowledge in various local restaurants on evenings and weekends. The realisation came that if he wanted to cook, he would have to get on a train at the age of 17 and head south. Today, you can travel to any county in the UK and find two or three really good restaurants. There is more variety than ever and plenty of skill out there. During Jones' apprenticeship there were very few places. John Burton-Race was at the very foundation of that early movement, alongside only a handful of other chefs including Nico Ladenis, Marco Pierre White, the Roux brothers and Raymond Blanc, all having trained brigades and who, in turn, went on to train the next generation. So it was that the culinary world spread from these roots.

17

A GOOD EGG

JONES'S BREAK came in a small restaurant in Rickmansworth where he was one of only three staff in the kitchen. It was a steep learning curve but a beneficial one, as he had to learn every aspect of food production. He left with a solid base and good overall knowledge of the workings of a kitchen. A stint followed at the Mountbatten Hotel in London's Covent Garden, training under a purely classical head chef. Spare time was consumed by picking up shifts at the renowned Waterside Inn, run by the legendary brothers Albert and Michel Roux. Back then, there were four or five standout restaurants and Jones wanted to work them all, including Le Gavroche and The Waterside.

Having worked a straight 10 days, Jones would spend his leisure time every second weekend at The Waterside Inn. 'It was great working in the late 1980s in that environment,' he says. 'Michel Roux Senior was in the kitchen. When you worked the front line, whether you cooked the fish or meat, Michel would always be a metre away or he would pass right in front of you, and he instilled a calm environment in the kitchen, although it was very intense. I loved working under Mark Dodson at that time. It was tough but I loved every second.'

Roux was quick to pick up on Jones's talent. Having started off on the fish, he ended on the sauce section — the holy grail of the kitchen and the one most people were scared of. Offered the position of chef de partie, he turned it down through regard for his then head chef at the Mountbatten, where he was still in employment. He had decided to stay on at the Mountbatten until he had completed a respectable 18 months at the hotel, continuing to work only part-time at The Waterside. The latter's kitchen proved to be tough going but as an aspiring 21-year-old, Jones was quick to knuckle down. Having worked his way through The Waterside's brigade, the same day Jones was offered the chef de partie position, he had been weighing up an offer to join Le Manoir on a trial basis. Told that he could start the following week, Jones penned a reply, stating that he could not take up the position for a further twelve months because he had just begun his dream job on sauce at The Waterside. Unbeknown to him, Clive Fretwell, head chef at Le Manoir, had rung The Waterside for a character reference. Jones would generally arrive at 6am, brew coffee and make toast. Michel Roux was never normally in the kitchen in the morning. He was that day … as soon as the fans went on. Roux immediately asked what the meaning of the letter was, to which Jones replied that it was in reference to the following year, not then and there. He had to reassure Roux he was not going anywhere for the duration. Three months later he was offered a sous chef's role at The Waterside but in typical fashion, he had already committed to Raymond Blanc at Le Manoir and turned it down. In Blanc's kitchen, which saw the likes of John Burton-Race, Michael Caines, Aaron Patterson and Clive Fretwell manning the stoves, he was keen to work on every section before taking on such responsibility. Despite having had an amazing experience at The Waterside, he knew he needed to learn more in a different kitchen and from a different master. A year later, he moved to Le Manoir.

With Fretwell at the helm as head chef and unlikely to move on any time soon, Jones decided it was time for him to take the next step in his career and he left Le Manoir having secured a position on Necker Island, the private luxury resort island owned by Richard Branson, who, at the time, was a part-owner of Le Manoir. A brief consultancy in the Maldives followed before he returned to the UK in 1996, where he took up a position at Homewood Park in Bath. Within two years, he earned his first Michelin star and four AA rosettes. The product of his own success, suddenly he found himself a much sought-after chef. He headed the kitchen at Waldo's, the renowned restaurant of Cliveden, a luxury country house hotel in Berkshire. Awarded his second star, another four AA rosettes and 8/10 in the Good Food Guide, it was not long before a certain Raymond Blanc showed up at the door, set on tempting his former employee back into the fold. There was little persuasion needed and in 1999 he was appointed Executive Head Chef at Le Manoir, having every year retained two Michelin stars, an achievement the restaurant has realised for more than 30 years, alongside earning the maximum five AA rosettes.

'The Manoir family is a fabulous thing Raymond has created over the years, and John Burton-Race is from that same family,' Jones tells me. 'He was one of the first people to hold a head chef position at Le Manoir. That is something he is immensely proud of, so when he comes back here I make sure that everyone shakes his hand and makes a fuss of him, because he is our history; he is part of what Raymond has created, not only for it being a great place, but also because John was part of spearheading a number of great chefs that went on to lead the way with their own Michelin stars.'

Paul Foster, of The Dining Room at Mallory Court, says of Jones, 'It was a fantastic experience and helped shape me into the chef I am today. I can still hear Gary Jones' voice in my head.' Agnar Sverisson, of Texture, describes how supportive Jones was when he was working at Le Manoir while trying to set up his own business. And Steve Love told The Caterer: 'He puts the emphasis on developing chefs. I learnt so much from watching him. People skills for one thing—I only ever saw him lose it twice and, yes, he still kept that pencil behind his ear.'

Despite the conflict at Petit Blanc, Blanc's friendship with John endured, as he tells me. 'I am very fond of John; he is a very good egg and a great craftsman. He was always very tough on himself, and he was never one to suffer fools easily. I am a control freak, but I can delegate. And that is where we are different. In a way, that was a fault of him not being patient because today especially, you need to be patient. We need to be much better teachers in order to bring new people to this industry. I was conscious of creating a better environment in the kitchen. John would sometimes only take things on himself and would get highly frustrated. He is hotheaded and he is what he is, but he is a good man. Every day I know how tough it is to cook for others, which is why I never criticise when others cook for me. You dream about food. You have nightmares about food. I gave John as much as I could because he was the type of person who just drank knowledge. In terms of technique he was a lot better than me, but he had a lot to learn about Frenchness. My mum and grandma were extraordinary cooks and even with all that DNA behind me, I was always open to new ideas. While my mum had a deep knowledge it was, however, mostly about generosity. The table was the most powerful medium in the house. It was where family and friends gathered, talked, laughed and argued while eating and enjoying beautiful food, what the earth had given us.' For Blanc, a restaurant and its food is all about warmth and true hospitality. "As a business I always want to share what I know, not educate people, but share my knowledge to enrich their lives. While I cannot talk for John, I enjoy what I am doing so much and what I enjoy the most is people and creating a whole environment which is not just about food."

18

L'ORTOLAN

L'ORTOLAN, IN Shinfield, near Reading, Berkshire, boasts a rich culinary history, with five Michelin starred chefs having graced its kitchen over the years. The former red brick vicarage in Church Lane was built in the mid-1800s and suffered fire damage during the Second World War, resulting in the destruction of the third floor. It became a private house from 1939 until 1978 when it opened as a restaurant by chef Richard Sandford, and eponymously named Milton Sandford. Having worked his way through a number of Parisian kitchens, Sandford brought his French influences to Berkshire, and was duly rewarded three years later when he gained a Michelin star in 1982 — one of only seventeen in the UK at the time. 'Fashionably decorated in light wood and pale tan paint with an abundance of fresh flowers everywhere, the comfortable bar offers a choice of aperitifs before you enjoy your meal,' noted The Country Guide to Hotels, Restaurants & Pubs in 1980. Nico Ladenis was the next chef to take over the property but left the re-named Chez Nico in only his second year, but not without having been rated two stars by the 1986 Michelin Guide and Egon Ronay's Lucas

Guide. He was to tell Caterer & Housekeeper, "One night I walked on to the stage, took a look at the audience and decided I didn't want to perform any longer. I thought this was the moment to bow out.'

It was also a light bulb moment for John Burton-Race, whose customers at Petit Blanc included Sir David Napley, who would travel from Beckonsfield two or three times a week to enjoy John's cuisine. Napley was a highly respected lawyer who came into the public spotlight for his groundbreaking work on a number of suspected miscarriages of justice, notably the one-armed bandit murder case in the early 1970s which inspired the film Get Carter. On one dining occasion Napley told John, 'If you ever want to get anywhere, let me know.' Conscious that numerous people had said the same thing to him over the years, John took it with the proverbial pinch of salt, having learned that when it comes to money, such promises invariably turn out to be false. Napley retorted, 'I don't know whom you think you are talking to, but the offer is on the table. If you take it, you take it, if you don't, you don't, it is no skin off my nose.' About a year later and with the thought of running his own establishment firmly fixed in his mind, John approached Napley and asked if he remembered the offer. Napley was pivotal in John's next career move, offering more guidance in how to run a business than he ever received from his previous employer. 'Raymond Blanc has subsequently been charming, which is what he does. He learnt to play the game but for a young man starting out, it would have been nice if he had been more supportive of me,' John tells me. 'Then again, if I think back to the fact that half his staff came to work for me when I left Le Petit Blanc, there is no reason why he should have been. When I said I wanted to leave and run my own restaurant, he didn't want me to go. However, his wife at the time, Jenny Blanc, couldn't stand me and in the end, I couldn't stand working for her. When I gained a Michelin star at Le Petit Blanc, she accused me of trying to kill the business. I took objection to that.' When a car turned up with one of Jenny's secretaries on board, John packed up his apron, wrapped it in brown paper and wrote a little message to Mrs Blanc, stating, 'You'll be needing this because you can cook.' He then phoned Raymond Blanc and resigned.

Napley was the type who could raise hundreds of thousands of pounds from a friend based on a single phone call, and happily bankrolled John just when he was in need of driving his career forward. With financial backing linked to Napley and a group of shareholders, John and his then wife Marie-Christine acquired the Shinfield property from Nico Ladenis in October 1986. The move from the Blanc stable fulfilled a lifelong dream for John to open his own restaurant. While he might not have been able to exorcise his inner demons, having his own kitchen offered him complete freedom of expression. Now he had a sanctuary where he could challenge orthodox ideas and where he was not afraid to experiment, reformulate and refine traditional dishes. Like a midwife, he would deliver different ideas through his menus, analysing ingredients before pooling them into refined elegance on a plate. He knew his destiny lay in no one else's hands but his own. With no one willing or daring enough to interrogate his actions, his outlook on food took on a whole new intensity, possibly fuelled by the mental and physical bruising he had endured as a child, manifesting in courage and iconoclastic tendencies.

Yes, there would be incendiary moments, lots of them, but that was all part and parcel of kitchen life at the time. But then John was not, and never will be, a man to compromise on his principals, but rather a renaissance man working in his own domain like a precision instrument; a complex but brilliant mind, channeling all his knowledge and strengths to deliver nothing short of excellence to his customers. This, in turn, created conflict between John and Marie-Christine, the one person who possessed the business brains and acumen. She had a habit of asking John how much things cost, to which he would lie, replying that he had no idea. Marie-Christine would then respond that he had better find out, or they would starve. So, what did he do? He made prices up. Marie-Christine would then add 25 per cent on top. The problem would not go away, however, because John was still not charging enough to cover both costs and make a profit. He was desperate to do everything all at once, and his boredom threshold was zero.

If, for example, he cooked a squab pigeon in a particular way and 60 diners liked it, he would get fed up with it and want to cook something else. His attitude was that he needed to push on, regardless of the financial implications. He had this mental and physical desire to continually achieve, and because he was still a relatively young man, he wanted to start winning all the gongs. The problem was that when he started winning, he realised it was not the gongs that were driving him. The simple fact was that he wanted to do more, to do better and to be different. Basically, he didn't know when to stop. At one point, L'Ortolan got up 800 bins on the wine list, equating to about £350,000 worth of paid stock. Not in a position to afford a second, his one and only drinks sommelier, who was being paid handsomely for his knowledge, would arrive at table and take the order, but then go downstairs and find the bottle. In any other high-end restaurant is a second sommelier to retrieve bottles, thereby keeping the main man on the floor.

Gary Jones was first to come across John Burton-Race at L'Ortolan and found him intense. This was an era when there was no censorship in the kitchen — none whatsoever. Jones, however, was already well versed in such tense scenarios, having worked with the Roux brothers in the late 1980s, when one would think to oneself, 'is this what happens? Okay. I can survive in these situations.' Ever the diplomat, and in whatever kitchen he found himself, Jones endeavoured to protect other people who found themselves in similar situations, by trying to minimise any kind of happenings in the kitchen he thought were unnecessary.

John Burton-Race, however, was on a single-minded mission and his relentless search for perfection was to gain him a Michelin star after just a year at L'Ortolan, followed by a second a year later. Marco Pierre White and John were the only ones being talked about in those days. It was all about who was going to get their third star first. John eventually decided to end that pursuit for the plain fact that he had run out of cash to spend on the building. Marco had a bigger wine list and the infrastructure. He was also based in London while John was in the country. Even today, John is not sure whether it was his lack of ability rather than his standing that the coveted third star eluded him. In a sense not earning it proved to be his biggest regret, because he had wanted to see how far how could go.

The search for perfection was both crazily pricey and relentless. The dress plates were engraved with the L'Ortolan bird logo at a cost of £100 each. For the place settings, John imported Christofle silver, seen only in the finest Parisian restaurants. He had glasses that cost a fortune but were broken all too frequently by diners or waiting-on staff. He took a dislike to the chairs he inherited with the restaurant so changed them. Neither was the table linen to his liking. He wanted the menus in unbleached raw paper, which felt like linen. That was all well and good until a diner would spill gravy. Delicate ornamental L'Ortolan birds were dotted throughout the restaurant but disappeared at an alarming rate into the handbags of female diners. Everything was nicked, including the silver salt and pepper mills, which cost £150 a set.

John's temple to his insanity was equally driving Marie-Christine insane. As the financial brains behind the business, she could see no way of stopping her husband's express train of desire to create this feeling of nothing being too much trouble. To John, everything was truly amazing, to the extent that he wanted to match the food that was coming out of the kitchen. Poor Marie-Christine bore the brunt of his manic passion. 'I think I sent her mad because it was a total battle, all the time,' he tells me. 'The reason our marriage collapsed was because I just didn't like or fancy her anymore, partly because she had turned from being my wife into my business partner. She was the one I argued with about everything we did.' The couple had married in the UK while John was working at Chewton Glen. Both sets of parents had tried to persuade them otherwise, to no avail.

19

A FAMILY AFFAIR

BORN INTO the hospitality business, Marie-Christine's extremely wealthy father and owned a 37-bedroom hotel and a couple of restaurants, and other family members owned restaurants in the south of France. Schooled in Honfleur, an enchanting city in the department of Calvados, in northern France's Normandy region, she gained distinctions in maths, and Marie-Christine's mastery of the English language was impeccable. With a working knowledge of Spanish and Italian, there was little wonder she shined front of house. While she possessed all the attributes that someone who ran a restaurant would want to employ, there was little wonder that Marie-Christine suffered equally under the pressure of the job at L'Ortolan, and even more so under the pressure of her husband—yet it was John who ended up despising her, seeing her as his enemy. When I asked John to elaborate on this, he tells me, 'If you have a restaurant manager and you speak to them badly, inevitably one of two things will happen. They will either have a fight with you or they will leave. It is different if you are married to that person, because they are not going anywhere, so you are almost worse off because at the back of your mind you know they are not going to simply throw in the towel. If you had a restaurant manager running the business for you front of house, you would have to think twice before opening your mouth for fear of ending up without a manager. I came from the school of hard knocks, and I mean hard knocks because of my upbringing, and my mother being as she was. In the kitchen, if someone made a mistake I could say, "Fuck off, you can leave" knowing I would have to work a bit harder, but with the knowledge that I could do his or her job until I could find someone else to replace them.'

At the time of John's estrangement from Marie-Christine, many young, aspiring chefs had little sense of responsibility, urgency or work ethic, which is why life in the kitchen was rarely without drama, flare-ups an occupational hazard. John could certainly cook and run a kitchen, but his man management skills were considerably lacking. Call it pressure or a problem with separating oneself from the occupation, but the requirements and responsibilities of running a great kitchen wore heavily on John's shoulders as he constantly strove for perfection. At L'Ortolan, he may have thought he had left behind the world of hard drinkers and drug users, dropouts and criminals, but he still had to put up with 'crap' from arrogant whippersnappers, often too big for their aprons. John's working environment was not somewhere he would tolerate either the shortcomings or insolence of his subordinates. A case in point was a young French chef John brought with him from the Blanc stable. The pair got on extremely well there but at L'Ortolan the young man became intolerable, to the extent that he was holding John back. Every time John had an idea and he wanted him to sort it out, he would agree and then nothing would happen. According to John, the attitude was, 'You fucking do it'. A red rag to a bull, you might think, and you would be right, because John got rid of him. The reality then hit, because once in pastry, where his previous employer had been stationed, John realised that he was possibly not up to the standard that his sacked employee had set. What did he do? A typical John Burton-Race stunt. He shoved all the menus in the bin and told his team he wanted it all changed. Understandably, everyone went mad. All the ideas that he had and that had been thrown back at him by his former employee were suddenly on the menu. Chaos ensued, with diners having to wait up to an hour for a pudding.

Despite all the comings and goings of staff, L'Ortolan was very much a family affair. Having completed his training at Le Manoir, John's brother Jamie moved to L'Ortolan as number two chef. 'All my life, I've been trying to find out what goes on inside James's head. He's a deep guy, loyal, hard-working and trusting. He's sound and secure but not emotional,' John told the Sunday Times Magazine in January 1999. 'I am emotional, fairly complex and quite demanding. He is sure-footed, strong, straight down the line, very solitary and very quiet. We're physically and mentally very different people and yet, because we've shared the same childhood, I can see characteristics in him — tolerance levels, attitudes to incompetence — which are mirrored in myself. But whereas you'll hear about it from me because I'll shout, you won't hear anything from him.'

Having worked with John at Quat'Saisons before Le Manoir existed, in the same position as sous chef, Nigel Marriage also joined John at L'Ortolan. After transferring to Le Manoir when John opened Le Petit Blanc, Marriage had thought cooking at a bistro below his station and wanted to better himself, so wrote to John for a position.

'John is a great chef and he cares about provenance and traceability. When he opened L'Ortolan I really was so happy for him, because at first there had been a frostiness between us,' Blanc tells me. 'I visited L'Ortolan and it was lovely. John was consummate professional, and he really wanted to succeed in his world of excellence. He also had the right approach because he was hard working, always demanding high standards that were all part of his character. He was a young Englishman with such extraordinary qualities.'

L'Ortolan was doing a dozen covers at lunch and up to 50 in the evenings. Sunday lunch reached the insanity stage. While John was to run the business for 14 years and it eventually became successful financially, for the first six years it washed its face but didn't make a pound. The private investors were not particularly phased, however, because they had been enjoying tax relief under the Business Expansion Scheme. Every time the Burton-Races had some money, John set about refurbishing, whether by changing carpets or marble plastering one of the walls. With the kitchen getting old, he would buy replacement equipment secondhand because he couldn't afford new.

If it hadn't been set up in the way it was by Sir David Napley, it would never have made sense. What it was bought for and what it eventually sold for made all the difference. John spent those 14 years buying out shareholders one by one. The more the shareholders saw that there was no chance of the business making any real money, the more they were happy to sell. At the outset there were 42 shareholders happy to bring diners along to 'their restaurant', even if they only had a stake which was worth one of the sofas; at that time, it was possible to buy in for as little as £1,500. There were a couple of shareholders with a £3,000 stake and one exception — Lady Cromwell, who had a £20,000 stake. John had an inherent fear of the annual general meetings, worried that the shareholders would target him and interrogate his actions, even though Sir David had a way of making gloom look good. In one particularly bad year, noticing that John looked more worried than usual and feeling yet again that he had let down the people who supported him, Lady Cromwell pulled him aside and said she didn't care what others thought. John was consistently turning out lovely food, she read about him every week and if he ever got really in the mire, he must ring her and she would put more money into the pot. John's answer to that was to forget the following five hours of purgatory and go mad in the kitchen.

Meanwhile, having emerged from The Waterside's three-star environment and moving across to Le Manoir, a young, buzzing Gary Jones continued learning, shifting in L'Ortolan's kitchen alongside Jamie. John, he recalls, did not hold back. 'He wanted his standards high and he could be very harsh as a result, because he wanted those standards maintained. Having said that, I have always found John to be great fun. His sense of humour is amazing and I have always enjoyed his warm, zany character. At L'Ortolan he was cooking some of the best food I have ever eaten.'

It was a tough kitchen to be in, but Jones wanted to absorb as much as possible during his time there. He clearly made an impression. Having spent a week's holiday period at L'Ortolan, at the end of the seven days and impressed with whatever he had done no matter what stick passed his way, John invited him for Sunday lunch. Aged 24, there was no way on his salary that he could otherwise afford Sunday lunch at L'Ortolan. No matter, Gary invited his girlfriend to join him and he remembers driving into the car park in his clapped-out 1969 flat screen VW Beetle, parking alongside the Bentleys, Rollers and Jags. He was understandably nervous because, like John, his comfort zone lay in the kitchen, the place of screaming and shouting and abuse, of cuts, burns and scars. They were the youngest couple there and Gary could not believe it when John cooked his heart out, preparing them dishes off the menu. As a result, they became the envy of the room. He did a fantastic Pescatery course; seven courses of pure magic.

'John has this reputation of being a hard taskmaster, but then he will invite you to Sunday lunch with your girlfriend and will go out of his way to make sure you have a fantastic time,' says Gary. 'I have never been on the wrong side of him, thank goodness. Having said that, there is a lovely warmth to him, but I think he has been hurt at some point and that comes out in the way he flips on occasion. When he comes to Le Manoir, I make sure everyone knows not only who he is, but also what a contribution he has made to Le Manoir. He is a legend in the industry.'

With L'Ortolan's brigade of ten dedicated chefs and two Michelin Stars to boast about, the little French bird was truly flying, with success swiftly followed by Three Star Egon Ronay, Five Star AA, 5/5 Good Food Guide, 17/20 Gault Milleau, Egon Ronay Restaurant of the Year, and Good Food Guide Country Restaurant of the Year.

20

MARRIAGE MADE IN HELL

JOHN'S NEMESIS at Le Manoir, a certain Nigel Marriage, had taken up a position as chef de cuisine. In 1993, the pair competed in the Culinary Olympics, representing Great Britain in Madrid against thirteen other nations, winning a silver two golds and a platinum medal for Best Chef. Today a renowned chef, Alan Murchison joined the team in 1996, working his way up to junior sous chef before leaving to take up a position at Le Manoir aux Quat'Saisons.

Marriage was renowned as being the mother of all madmen, according to John, and 'completely bonkers, but I loved him to bits.' Marriage was working in constant pain, most likely as a result of contracting polio as a child. He walked with a limp and was the scourge of any kitchen where he worked. The only way he could keep circulation in his legs was to rise at a ridiculous hour in the morning, get on a racing bike, wear himself out and then cover a 14-hour shift. Even so, Marriage's behaviour was intolerable. 'He would grab people by the neck and chuck them around, and finally it had to come to an end,' John tells me.

Michel Roux Senior remembers the occasion when one of his chefs from The Waterside went to L'Ortolan to work but could not stay. He said it was a madhouse because of the sous chef—a certain Nigel Marriage. The problem was that it was happening when John was there, and it was down to him to control the situation. It didn't help when a television documentary was made of life in the kitchen, featuring the tyrants that stalked the ovens, and the stresses and strains of everyday kitchen life, including the likes of Marriage, John and Marco Pierre White. John remembers it well. 'Half of the young guns we had worked for previously were certainly worse than us, treating us really badly. On television, however, they dumped us right in it, accusing us of being insane, physically violent, abusive bullies, so as the next generation of chefs, we were disgraced in front of the public.'

The year was 1995, and one evening a particular incident in the L'Ortolan kitchen passed into culinary folklore. While the restaurant did 63 covers, the kitchen was not as organised as it normally was. John was working on fish while sous chef Marriage was dependent on a young French commis called Otis for the sauce. The young lad had only been in the kitchen for three months and was wet behind the ears. He was shy and nervous but keen to impress his seniors, including Marriage, who never took prisoners. After a good start to the evening, things went wrong and service crumbled. Tempers rose and the heat in the kitchen increased. John ranted at Marriage, who in turn spat forth venom to anyone who dared come close enough. Poor Otis came into his line of fire, but sadly for him, had been the root of the problem throughout the evening. He got a bollocking, followed by a thump. The kitchen was in a mess: orders were not going out as they should, and Otis was in the corner, cowering like a scalded lamb. Chef was shouting at him for Foie Gras. John's stomach was in turmoil. Marriage was at boiling point, a pressure cooker ready to blow. He went behind Otis, kicked him in his heel and drew an imaginary line across the floor. 'Cross it and you're a dead Frenchman. I will bung you out the fucking window.' It was meant to be a joke, sort of, but it was not taken that way. John tried to calm the situation. He then drew a line with his foot and told Otis not to step outside of his box. Candid camera time. The film crew had primed a couple of stagiaires under false pretences with cameras. Working for free, in another chef's kitchen, what did they care what they filmed? When John saw the film later, he laughed. He was the only one that did. Everyone watching it at home was outraged. The situation was not helped when the film crew shot John as this opulent bloke driving in his Porsche, so everybody who didn't have the money for a bicycle suddenly hated him. All the upper-crusties who thought John Burton-Race was politically correct, brilliantly talented and fun to be with suddenly didn't like him anymore because they felt he had let them down. It was probably fortunate that by then most of the shareholders had been bought out.

With the public offered front row seats to L'Ortolan kitchen's explosive pressure cooker environment, in no small thanks to those undercover cameras, the Press was quick to inject its own dose of vitriol. It has to be said that it was not of John's doing, but he was the one impaled. In itself an isolated incident, the travesty was that from this point on, it stuck. Suddenly we had John Burton-Race the madman rather than John Burton-Race the kitchen supremo. The incident prompted a demand for tough new rules to stamp out violence in kitchens. It was not only John's kitchen that caught the flak, however. The Big Story on ITV had also planted secret cameras in the kitchens of L'Escargot in London's Soho, capturing examples of verbal and physical abuse dished out to a kitchen porter by head chef Gary Hollihead. The Caterer, the industry flag bearer, was inundated with telephone calls and letters condemning the chefs' behaviour. John was quickly on the defensive, telling The Caterer he 'very much regretted' the behaviour filmed in his kitchen and that he had spoken to the individuals, concerned, emphasising that such behaviour was unacceptable. On the night of the incident, John called Marriage into his office and demanded an explanation for his actions. 'The service is crap, you cooked like a prick. Everything was wrong, garnishes were missing. Otis was an idiot and you start tapping him, the whole thing went to pieces,' he told The Caterer. Nigel was reprimanded a second time and John told the team that this was ever going to happen again, ever. 'I have also since addressed all my staff and made it clear that conduct of this sort will not be tolerated,' he commented. Otis remained in employment, and, in fact, was scheduled to work with Nigel Marriage at a cooking demonstration at the Sunday Times Festival of Food and Wine at Olympia. Raymond Blanc was also quick to react to the programme's revelations, telling The Caterer: 'Violence is a criminal offence and people should speak out against it,' although he did go on to admit that he had been aggressive in the past. The previous year, The Caterer had carried out a survey which revealed 18 per cent of staff involved in food preparation had been physically abused at work.

John did not believe for a moment that the incident was premeditated, but that it was more a question of control and Marriage had clearly lost it. When John watched it again, having taken the backlash, he was disgusted although he had experienced far worse in the kitchen during his career. The film didn't in any way portray the man he was or what he stood for. He told The Caterer that he didn't see the act as a serious, malicious or vindictive attack, and that he thought Marriage was possibly sorry for his actions.

Writing in the Daily Telegraph in August 2000 while reviewing John's food at The Landmark Hotel, where John was later to run his eponymous restaurant, Matthew Norman noted: 'Chief villain was the sous chef Nigel Marriage, a brutish fellow with a televised penchant for reducing terrified French boys to tearful jellies with his words and boots. Although Mr Burton-Race himself was filmed doing no more than a bit of yelling, and later explained that he'd spoken to everyone concerned about their behaviour, he suffered some awful fallout from this programme—bad luck, one suspects, on someone believed to be among the better natured of our top chefs. Perhaps the memory of this exposure to the gamma rays of public attention partly explains the low-key opening of this new London venture, or perhaps he just wants to build the business quietly.'

As far as John was concerned and despite what the public perception was, the industry was not run by a bunch of foul-mouthed, yobbo-type bully boys. The incident prompted Kit Chapman from the Castle Hotel in Taunton to call for a code of conduct and disciplinary procedures in the catering industry. As far as John was concerned, you could create all the guidelines you wanted, but the difference between the man at the top of his profession and the man selling hotdogs at a burger stall were light years apart. 'Find me a guy that's never, ever tapped someone on the arm, kicked someone up the bum, sworn at them. I'd be surprised. I'm not a saint. Who is?'

I ask Gary Jones for his views on the issue of bullying in kitchens. 'Chefs then worked hard and played hard, and there is still an element of that, but we just have to be a bit more responsible in terms of our public persona. How many phones are there in any given day in the kitchen, and how many people can record you? There are lots of traps out there for you to be caught out.'

When Jones was picking up casual shifts at L'Ortolan, he found Marriage to be particularly unhelpful. 'I was at L'Ortolan, unpaid, trying to learn as much as possible. If, for example, I had finished a task, I would approach Nigel and ask what needed doing. His response would be, "If I fucking need something from you, I will ask". I was not going to let that get me down, because I had seen that approach before. I would jump in and help someone prep a rabbit. Because I had worked in some great kitchens, no one could prep a rabbit faster or better than me. If I saw someone making an error, I felt it was necessary for me to pass my skill on. Maybe Nigel's attitude was such because it was the way he had been treated in kitchens, but thankfully I am of an age now where these things are no longer tolerated in the industry. The Nigel Marriage years were harsh for everybody there.'

While chefs tried their best to create an environment of positivity, learning and showing people the way, tempers would more often than not become frayed. 'I never copied or mirrored what I saw. Rather, I wanted to know the techniques, flavours and food combinations,' Jones tells me. 'I wanted to work with the best chefs in Great Britain at the time. John was one of them and I had to get into his kitchen. Working in a kitchen is a pressured environment but I believe it is important to analyse the individuals you are training, to look into their family backgrounds and see how they had been treated. During my training, there was a fear of losing standards which caused people to act in a certain way. I admit that at the time it was a brutal environment to work in. Today at Le Manoir we have 40 chefs and we are doing 80 covers. Back then we had 13 chefs doing 100 covers, so it required from 6am to 1am or 2am to get through the day. The standards were high and therefore there was no let-up in order to maintain those standards. Raymond has played no small part in making the changes happen, which is why I have such great admiration for him.'

When John and Marriage worked for Raymond Blanc, their relationship had been completely hostile. 'We were both sous chefs. I would be making something and turn away, and he would come along from his section, dump a load of sauce in what I was preparing, and then call Raymond over and ask him if he had tasted my sauce. On one particular night, I was working on station when a chef called Dominic came across from pastry with some soufflés and opened my oven door from between my legs, because he didn't have an oven in his section. Nigel was on garnishes and fish and was giving me shit. The worst thing that can happen when you get to know me is when I go quiet, because you know I am going to blow. It's not when I am shouting—it's when I don't. I grabbed Marriage, dragged him out through the back door and pushed him into the dustbins. From that day forward he liked me. I had been there six months and he probably thought I was trying to get his job, but that was not the case.'

Marriage contacted John as soon as he moved to L'Ortolan, followed by the pastry chef and the rest of the team. In the end he could not afford all of them, despite the fact they all wanted to work with him. Those early days at L'Ortolan were a steep learning curve, and John remains particularly grateful for the support afforded him by Michel Roux Senior at The Waterside. In fact, Roux initially recommended him to Raymond Blanc, thereby helping him secure a position. Roux helped John source suppliers, and it was never an issue to pick the phone up and ask for advice. Roux would occasionally go for dinner and never pay a penny. Forever charming, he would introduce John to the inner circle. New to the Michelin fold, John would travel to Cannes for get-togethers but would miss the seminars because he was normally nursing a hangover.

L'Ortolan's lunch menu changed on a daily basis. Diners would sit down to a treat of escalope of tuna marinated in lime, the flesh and milk of fresh coconut, ginger and cumin same, with a light curry sauce made from the marinade. John and Marriage formed a seamless bond, each knowing what the other was thinking often before a move had been executed. Marriage told Fiona Sims, of Caterer and Hotelkeeper, in 1994, that he always knew what John was going to do before he did it. 'In the kitchen on a Saturday night it can get quite scary. You have to have total concentration. I have to know what he's just about to do and how it works—he'll look at the board and I already know what he's reading, know what he's about to call next … chef gets a bit depressed. I can always tell, so I try and dig him out. How? I start talking about food.

I never complain about anything, I never ask for a pay rise. John gives me money when it's due. If the food's good, that's the driving force. Second Chef. Second best? No. Not at all. Not here. I suppose most sous chefs want to open their own restaurant one day. I look at this place and I think this is all I want in life. I am really happy to see people out and enjoying their food. If they say the food's not good, I get upset, John gets upset. The carrot is Michelin. Three stars are what they want and nothing or nobody will stand in their way. If John said, "sorry Nigel, your sauces aren't three stars—you have to go", he would do it.'

For John, as chef-patron, it was a manic schedule. He slept a maximum of three hours a night. Close to burnout, his doctor warned that if he did not slow down, he would pay for it later in life. Taking no heed, it cost him dearly years later. At L'Ortolan, he would get up, have a cigarette, down a coffee, have another cigarette, and two more coffees. He was caught in the trap of being motivated by his own ego and ambition, and then there were the character assassinations to contend with. He had become a constantly moving target for a media happy to take potshots at a stereotypical chef in the prime of his life and who at any one time was seen as creative, inspired, energised, original and reactive. It was not so much an assault on his artistic creativity, which remained untainted, as his explosive encounters in the kitchen, something that Michel Roux Senior alludes to when I meet with him at The Waterside Inn in Bray. The revered French-born chef and restaurateur tells me a number of his diners had mentioned John's name to him, so out of curiosity he thought he would pay L'Ortolan a visit.

'John was concentrating on what I would call the exceptional, trying to achieve the maximum impact, yet he did not know what that was because he was too young at the time. The problem is that if you focus on something and the target is not totally known, then you are not going to help either yourself or others. He has never been an easy guy, simply because he is a perfectionist. We could hear his voice in the kitchen from the dining room on a few occasions. But then he had a sous chef who was worse than he was, a little bit of a crazy man. I think things were flying in that kitchen sometimes and that is not how you run a kitchen.' Vocal antics aside, Roux was extremely impressed with the food he was served. 'It is no good to go overboard or go crazy over some small detail, because what John was doing ranged from good to excellent. It was a one-star Michelin restaurant for a while. I had been there at least four times for a meal over the course of a few years and most of the time I would say what John was serving was more two-star than one. Today he is a very sensible person; a very good professional who has learned by his mistakes. He hasn't done many, but he has done a few. I think he knows that. If I was to say anything about him, it would be that if he had been a bit more rational then we would have been good friends, but to me he was too irrational because of his temper and because he was targeting something but he didn't know what. He is someone who wants the best and that is commendable, because in today's world not too many people want that. John can be an inspiration for young people, especially now because he has calmed down, because quite a lot of young people have been very good in the trade, Marco Pierre White being one, but he was a little bit crazy, like John.'

Roux's nephew, Michel Roux Junior, a highly accomplished chef and television luminary in his own right, says the one thing about John Burton-Race is that he is a damned good chef—something I came to expect to hear from any number of chefs I spoke with. 'He can cook as well as any other chef I know,' he tells me. 'His taste is unbelievable, and his passion is second-to-none, and that is part of his problem because he remains over-exuberant and passionate in anything he undertakes, and that takes priority over anything else. Although I don't think he has a bad bone in him, he probably wonders why he gets into so much trouble.'

Michel Roux Junior runs the highly respected Le Gavroche in London's Upper Brook Street, Mayfair, having carved a name for himself thanks to the major influences of his father Albert and Uncle Michel. Growing up in the countryside, from the age of 13 he was in the kitchen cleaning pots and pans during school holidays to earn extra pocket money, so the value of work and money were certainly instilled in him from an early age. He has been at the helm of Le Gavroche since 1989, the restaurant having opened originally in 1967 and run by his father. Similar to John, there are many things that still drive him and make him jump out of bed in the morning before the alarm has rung; seeing the next generation of chefs being passionate about what they do and being able to teach them not just cooking skills, but also life skills, essential things that they will remember 20 years on. 'The creativity comes and goes. What is nice is to sit down and eat new dishes with the head chefs and sous chefs and discuss the menu. It is important to get the team involved, especially as I am not here every single day of the year. They have to feel they are an integral part of every dish that goes out. It is a life of juggling and prioritising and I am sure that John knows that only too well.'

Although never having worked the kitchen alongside John, Michel Roux Junior has bumped into him several times at events. Having enjoyed two meals at L'Ortolan, he found the food to be 'truly amazing'. It was the beginning of an era in the country where British chefs were finally being recognised, and John was one of the leaders and really making his mark. Every young chef wanted to be the next John Burton-Race or work with him, as they really saw him as a leader. John was like the Marco Pierre Whites and Gordon Ramsays of this world, who drew attention to themselves but for all the right reasons. The bad news and the noise came later. 'Rumour has it that when John blew a fuse, boy did he blow, but I can't say because I have never worked with him the kitchen,' says Michel Roux Junior. 'Personally, I have always had a soft spot for him, as have many others in the industry. Yes, he has been a little bit of a naughty boy in terms of relationships but then look at my dad. He has probably had more headlines than John in that respect! I don't know who advises John, or indeed if he does take advice, but he does seem to make bad or strange decisions, but then he has always had itchy feet, in that he does not like to stay put for too long. He likes challenges, and maybe that stems from his childhood when he was always on the move. On a personal note I do not have a bad thing to say about him because I love his food, his exuberance and his passion, and at the end of the day he has probably been a little bit misunderstood.'

21

DINING OUT ON PSYCHOSIS

AROUND THE same period John was making waves at L'Ortolan, one of his contemporaries, Martin Blunos, had created Lettonie in Bristol. Having opened as chef and owner alongside his then girlfriend Sian (later to become his wife) in 1988, the Franco-British style of cooking with Eastern European overtones earned him a Michelin star a year later and a second in 1991. Blunos went on to hold his two Michelin stars for 15 years. Unlike some of his peers, he attended college in Cheltenham before working a spell at the Strand Palace Hotel in London. Then followed a season in Switzerland and numerous cruises on a Greek tycoon's yacht before landing a role at Lampwicks in London's Battersea Road, where the main competition came from Nico Ladenis during his early nouvelle cuisine phase. Blunos recalls receiving his second star at Lettonie. It was leaked and Marco Pierre White rang to relay the good news and he didn't believe him. Notification arrived the following day. A pat on the back from his peers, he was now in an elite group, with only 11 two stars in the country at that time. Lettonie had no driveway and no lounge; it was most certainly not Le Manoir but rather a part of a row of shops with a veterinary practice on one side and a dry cleaner on the other, and diners had to pull up on the street.

Blunos was awarded his crystal by Pierre Koffman, the French-born chef who was one of a handful in the United Kingdom to have been awarded the coveted three Michelin stars at his restaurant La Tante Claire in London. Interestingly, with Michelin, on each occasion that the embargoed list is leaked, chefs tend not to look at who has won a star but rather who has lost one. Paul Heathcote, at the eponymously named Heathcotes, in Preston, received two stars the same year as Blunos. Heathcote, today a chef, restaurateur and food consultant, spent two years under the guidance of Raymond Blanc at Le Manoir aux Quat'Saisons. Prior to this he worked at the Connaught Hotel in London in 1983, having joined Michel Bourdin's 50-strong brigade of highly disciplined classical French cooks. He told The Guardian: 'They made you go through every single process and not cut any corners. It was a meticulously hard school, there's no question about it. But I learned an enormous amount there.' Joining Le Manoir in 1985, which had an impressive kitchen garden supplying the restaurant, Heathcote says he developed a passion for fresh produce, telling The Independent: 'It wasn't uncommon to be out in the vegetable garden digging up baby leeks and carrots at 8pm.'

Heathcote opened his eponymous restaurant in 1990 aged 29. The place had only been trading nine days when a gas leak caused the kitchen to go up in flames. A mere two days later, it re-opened. His first Michelin star in 1992 was followed with the award of Good Food Guide's Restaurant of the Year and a second star in 1994, which he retained for the next four years. Heathcotes remained a one-star establishment until 2003 when it was re-launched as the Longridge Restaurant, regaining its second star in the 2004 awards.

Martin Blunos recalls when his wife Sian fell pregnant with their first child and ended up doing fish prep between bouts of morning sickness. She would then freshen up and go front of house. As she blossomed, Blunos employed a chef to take over her station. Following the births of their second son and a daughter, Coco, the couple thought it time to hang up their aprons at Lettonie. The fact that their living quarters were above the restaurant created numerous problems for the family, as people would occasionally knock at the door or ring the bell, resulting in them having to appear at least half decent all the time in order to show potential diners round. Once free of the restaurant shackles, Blunos slopped around in a T-shirt and shorts, open a can of Stella whenever he fancied and read The Times. If the phone rang, the majority of the time he wouldn't bother to answer. Sian completed a degree in nutrition and later wrote a book on baby food entitled Cooking For Coco. Sadly, with Blunos earning a crust on consultancy work, the marriage hit the rocks. 'Things happen for a reason, good or bad, things simply get in the way,' he tells me.

In 2016, Blunos became executive chef for Bespoke Hotels, and was based initially at The Talbot Inn in Ripley, Surrey. A year later he took the bold decision to ditch his fine dining and Michelin stars for a new life in Bangkok, where he opened the eponymously named Blunos. Housed on the 14th floor of the four-star Eastin Grand Hotel Sathorn, the restaurant took over the space vacated by Luce, an Italian. Floor-to-ceiling windows look out on the adjacent swimming pool, where the poolside bar has resident DJs spinning upbeat music.

I caught up with him at the Talbot Inn while he was enjoying a brief vacation in the UK. I expected to pinpoint Mr Blunos with his famously impressive walrus moustache and his blond hair in a ponytail, but instead he was sporting a fresh, streamlined look—despite having once said that if he ever got short hair he would remove his moustache, as he was concerned it would leave him looking like a member of Village People. I am pleased to report there is still a touch of zaniness in his character. He is known to wear Union Jack trousers at work at Blunos, a trait his Asian clientele love. He begins by telling me that it was Sian who knew of John before him. They met while John was working as a junior sous chef at La Sorbonne in Oxford where Sian was a commis chef, having just finished college. John took her under his wing.

Martin was first to meet John at L'Ortolan, when Nigel Marriage was also in the kitchen. He recalls them as being like chalk and cheese; both being a touch psychotic but good foils for each other. 'John is a good teacher,' he says. 'We all know he got caught out with the cameras, but that was down to Nigel. It is strange because if you were in any other industry and you were like that, Human Resources would be jumping all over you and you would end up in court. If you are in an office and you start abusing somebody and put him or her up against a filing cabinet, it is definitely frowned upon, but at that time in kitchens it was the norm. As you get older you start to realise you get a lot more out of people if they like you than if they are scared of you. These people create great food, but they are scared shitless. That pinch of love is the ingredient you cannot buy. There is this hidden ingredient, such as with grandmother's apple pie. It tastes beautiful because she doesn't cook for profit or margins—she cooks for her family because she loves them. In the kitchen, because you get angry and upset, you die a bit every day with all the stress. If something is wrong and the customer complains they think the chef is shit, but they don't realise there might be six or seven guys in the kitchen and any one of those can fuck up, but they blame you, so you take it very personally. The best restaurant is one where just you and I are cooking, but that's not a business. When you have 20 or 30 people and you have two sittings, and you have a pastry section, which is remote, you have to trust people. It is down to how you train and inspire and mentor them, because the beautiful thing about this wonderful human race is that we are all different. Thank goodness we are, because just imagine if we were all the same, if everyone was like John, what a horrible world that would be!' It is worth pointing out at this juncture that Martin Blunos and John Burton-Race remain the best of friends, so tongue-in-cheek throwaways are allowable.

One summer's day Martin and Sian took the train from Bristol to enjoy a meal at L'Ortolan. They sat under an oak tree and enjoyed possibly the best meal they had ever eaten. Martin remembers an amazing sweetbread dish with almonds, creamy in the middle, and he thought about the simplicity of the food but how it was so professional in its execution. 'I wondered how, in one way, John could appear so aggressive and then create something so beautiful, almost feminine in its elegance.' Having enjoyed the meal and copious amounts of wine, Martin and Sian were in no fit state to board a train back to Bristol. Generous to a fault, John paid for a taxi from Reading. Martin fell asleep in the back.

After that first enjoyable encounter, the couple returned on a number of occasions to dine at L'Ortolan before John and Martin were to enter the World's Best Fish Dish Competition, for which John prepared a lobster thermidor, a creamy mixture of cooked lobster meat, egg yolks and brandy stuffed into a lobster shell. Martin did 'something with elvers', which was all very West Country. Spending their leisure time together, Martin was taken with John's stories and humour, which he found infectious. 'The thing with John is that sometimes you don't know where you stand. Is he pissed off or is he just being normal? He can be quite cutting but actually that is quite refreshing because he doesn't suck up to anybody. He says it how he sees it, right or wrong. We all know it hasn't all been rosy for him. He has been an arsehole and John will be the first to admit that. In all my years of knowing him—and I have seen him when he is up and indestructible like Mr. Teflon, and when he is down and he has nothing—he always seems to come up smelling of roses, no matter how many times he has fallen into the shit, because he has that kind of character. He doesn't suffer fools. He is very opinionated and that gets him by, especially in this industry. Out of all the guys who have done a bit of crossover, John has always bounced back to his original love, cheffing, where he feels safe. He can be very dry, with that typically British sarcastic edge and just enough lilt that is funny, and you either get it or you don't. If you don't, you think he is a bit aggressive and hard, but it is just his demeanor.'

Martin and John would look forward to the Michelin dinners run by G.H. Mumm, one of the world's largest champagne producers. Martin became friends with Marie-Christine and the Burton-Race's children Naomi and Max, although Sian knew them even better because she and Marie-Christine once shared a place together. Chefs would dress in black ties and, in the company of their wives would begin the evening with a few glasses of champagne. By the end of the evening, half cut, truths would out—whether it be the VAT bill that they couldn't afford or the staff who had walked, and they would ending up thinking it was just the same shit, but in a different locality. To some chefs it must have been akin to therapy, because they would use the opportunity to unload on their friends. With the likes of John and Marco Pierre White, the driving forces of the new breed of outstanding chefs, Martin Blunos was flying under the radar. Despite his two stars at Letonnie, no one knew really who he was because he hadn't worked his way through the Raymond Blanc or Nico Ladenis stables.

It was an extraordinary time. Unlike in America, where if you were good at something you were seen to be aspirational, in the United Kingdom it was more the viewpoint of 'I can do that crap' and suddenly the knives would come out. John had become a victim of that culture, especially when it came to his private life.

From a very early age, John, pictured aged five, was to form a particularly close bond with his sister Clare, aged four. Born prematurely, she was such a tiny bundle that John later nicknamed her Diddy.

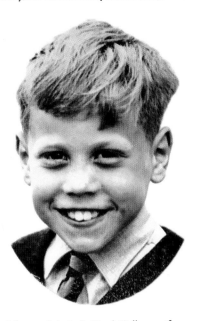

ABOVE: John, aged six, in St Mary's College uniform.

RIGHT: Clare aged 14. For as long she could remember, her brother was always the perfectionist in the kitchen.

Wild, single-minded and single-tracked, you might understandably presume that John, pictured sea fishing at Slapton Sands in 2007, has breezed through life with reckless abandon, in harness with a sense of purpose and vigour, forever wanting to be the best that can be.

John enjoying a day's fishing on holiday with Suzi in Tobago in 2007.

John's wife Suzi enjoying time out on holiday in Greece in 2005.

Suzi with Pip, aged two, on Flurrie, at Bearscombe, Devon, in 2006. No Health and Safety then!

John on fatherly duties with Pip in front of the London Eye in 2007, when he was taking part in Britain's Best Dish.

Pip in 2007, on an egg hunt.

John and Pip on tractor duty in the garden at Asherne Cottage, Strete, in 2007.

John and Suzi's wedding day (left to right): Chris Cook, Susie (maid of honour), Suzi, Pip, John, Anne, Louis and Ed Baines (best man).

Pip in the kitchen of the family home in Burlestone with Fanny the Terrier.

Summer garden table. When the Burton-Races cannot get to their beloved Provence, they bring France to Devon.

John Burton-Race is a man who has always been in charge of his own destiny, that which lay in his own hands and abilities. ©MATT AUSTIN

John remains one of the true edifices of culinary expertise; talk about food and his eyes light up. The enthusiasm for the subject matter simply pours forth. ©MATT AUSTIN

In a contemplative mood, John remains passionately driven by cooking, and appreciates the fact he is in a job in which he can become totally absorbed. ©MATT AUSTIN

Up early and out late, John Burton-Race is still living life at 100 miles an hour… although he still finds time for the occasional coffee break at home. ©MATT AUSTIN

Gary Jones: 'The word legend can be overused, but John Burton-Race truly is one. He was always on my list as part of my education to get to where I am today.'

"A Recipe has no love in it - as the cook, you bring that ingredient"

Martin Blunos

Michael Caines: 'John is a fighter. He doesn't give up, he is controversial, but then that is good because it makes him interesting. He is also outspoken, so he is worth listening to, but there is also a great depth of knowledge.'

Michel Roux Junior: 'I do not have a bad thing to say about John because I loved his food, his exuberance and his passion, but he has probably been a little bit misunderstood.' ©ISSY CROKER

Michel Roux Senior: 'John is what I would call someone who wants the best and that is commendable, because in today's world not too many people want that.' ©MARTIN BROGDALE

Raymond Blanc: 'During our time together I gave John as much as I could because he was the type of person who just drank knowledge. In terms of technique he was a lot better than me, but he had a lot to learn about Frenchness.'

Stephen Humphreys (pictured when he was one of three winners on the day at the Elior Culinary Competition, when his main course at the banquet was voted Diners' Choice) says of his friend: 'John is one of the nicest guys you could ever hope to meet. He would do absolutely anything for his friends and he is a very clever guy. In my eyes he is like the godfather of cooking.'

22

LENNY HENRY: CHEF!

HAVING ACHIEVED success in the 1993 Culinary Olympics representing Great Britain with Nigel Marriage, that same year John taught the actor and comedian Lenny Henry in the techniques of cookery for the BBC sitcom Chef!. Lenny and his then wife Dawn French lived close to L'Ortolan and became regular customers. Dawn became godmother to John and Marie-Christine's daughter Naomi and although everyone got on well, she went off John big time when he and his wife divorced, telling him what a despicable bloke he was. 'I went to Naomi's wedding in Paris and Dawn was there, and because she was happier with her new man, she treated me very pleasantly,' John tells me. 'To be perfectly honest, I was the one who was standoffish, not her, because I had taken the wrath of her mouth about 10 years before.'

Created and primarily written by Peter Tilbury, who wrote Birds Of A Feather, Chef! starred Lenny Henry as the tyrannical Gareth Blackstock. The show was popular and ran from 1993 to 1996 for 20 episodes over three series, with John as food consultant. Lenny's character allowed absolutely nothing to interfere with his pursuit of culinary excellence and he took to the role like a duck to, well, the oven. Although Lenny was trained in L'Ortolan's kitchen, the restaurant was modelled on Le Manoir aux Quat'Saisons and many scenes were filmed there.

Tilbury would dine at L'Ortolan and John recalls his particularly dry sense of humour. 'I used to talk to him, and we used to get pissed, and the more I got pissed the more I talked,' says John. 'It didn't seem to matter whether the stories were entirely true or slightly exaggerated; Peter would take it all on board. Then I didn't see him for two or three months and I thought maybe he'd had a bad meal or something. He then rang and said he wanted to come for a coffee, saying he had a great idea and he wanted me to be the consultant on this programme he was planning. He said if I didn't mind, he was going to exaggerate some of my stories, and I replied that that would be difficult. He said it wouldn't be and asked me to recount as many funny stories as I could remember, so I gave him a load more, and then still a load more. That was it until a year later when Peter contacted me again. We agreed a figure and got Lenny in the kitchen.'

Initially, the plan was to have the comedian at L'Ortolan for three weeks, where John would teach him the basics. Give him some pastry, get him to roll it out and dust it off and pretend that he knew what he was talking about. When Lenny arrived the first morning, all the lads saw this big, charismatic guy stroll in with his mock Caribbean voice booming, 'Hey man, what's happening? I'm going to show you how to cook.' John told him to shut the fuck up. He was there to show Lenny a few manoeuvres so it looked like he could cook, but there would be no showing off. Half joking, John told him he had entered what was a serious business, and so it began. By the end of the second service the following evening, Lenny confessed that every part of his body ached. While all the chefs had been running around sweating and screaming, our Lenny was shattered.

The next day he complained of feeling unwell and failed to show. Peter then came to see John and explained that Lenny was finding it difficult. John's response was to tell him that he needed to convey how physically draining the job was. 'If you like it or love it you will do it,' was John's response. 'If you are worried about your thighs and your calves, you are sweating and tired, the mental strain of it all is getting to you, and you are worried about how long everything takes to prepare, then no amount of adrenalin will get you through it. You will hate it, no matter what it gives in return.' By way of further explanation, he tells me about when he took up temporary residency at an inn close to his home in Devon in 2018. 'When I went to this pub it was dark when I arrived, and it was dark when I left. I never saw the fucking daylight for three-and-a-half months but it didn't matter, because the most important thing to me was whether I had enough time to make the frangipane for the apple tart, as well as doing all the other stuff. I was thinking that my aspiring young chef Harrison was not coming in to help me today, and I was conscious of how many diners had booked in, so I was in the zone again, on the job at hand and not worrying about anything else out there in the great big wide world. It's a form of hiding. You simply put your head down in your work and you give what you have got, with no clue about what anyone else is doing. Then when you are back home and you turn the television on late at night, and people are moaning about having to work 40 hours a week and can only take every other weekend off, of course you have no sympathy because you cannot relate to a large percentage of the public in jobs they don't really want to do, but they have to because they need to get the money in.'

Basically, when a chef is in this different place of madness, this place of gastronomy, it's all-consuming. It is not alcohol. It is not drugs. John is happy to leave all that well alone. In fact, with his personality, he would probably explode. 'Cooking is something you get sucked into. Even if you get tired easier and you are getting older, the minute you are in the kitchen you become a different person because you are totally involved in your job. You just want everything to be the best. Even if it is just a shepherd's pie in a pub, you know you are not going to overcook the lamb and you know you want to make a proper stock. If I am doing a potato, I want it to taste like one. People often ask me what is frying. Frying is cooking a crust, whether it is in batter or not around the item that you are frying at 180 degrees. The inside of whatever you are cooking is now getting hot, because what cooks the fish or potato is the steam created by its own natural juices. It depends in what oil you cook in, what has a higher temperature of burning and how many times you can use a particular oil. Then people look at me and think I am mad—it is only a fucking chip. If we go to the pub, it's about how much do we pay and what level the skill is. I will become your worst enemy if we are going to have a £150-a-head meal in a two-star Michelin restaurant anywhere in the world and it's not lovely or technically good. I am not talking about the artistry or the chef's particular style of cooking. I am talking about the technical skill of the cook, because that is what I am there for.'

Sunday Express Classic magazine noted in December 1994 that 'John Burton-Race is the workaholic, blessed with a sharp sense of humour, who provided the role model for the fictitious Gareth Blackstock, brilliantly portrayed on television by Lenny Henry.' Having taken a crash course in kitchen drama at John's double Michelin-starred restaurant, John said Lenny Henry was quick to learn. 'He now knows how to cook several dishes from start to finish. He learned skills like chopping vegetables at speed without looking. We have him all the rotten jobs! We'd say, "purge this snail Lenny" or "gut this rabbit".' Arrogant, tyrannical, talented and obsessive, Lenny as Blackstock could not have had a better role model than John Burton-Race as he served his diners traditional French cuisine with eclectic flair at Le Chateau Anglais.

The first episode of Chef! was developed over two years, which gave Lenny and writer Peter Tilbury plenty of time to discuss Blackstock's character motivation. Should the character be such an arsehole? Is this the right kind of character for Lenny to portray? Once that was ironed out and they greenlit the series, Tilbury had something like eight or nine weeks to write the rest. Addressing Janice, Blackstock's long-suffering wife and the one holding the purse strings, he said, 'I don't know whether you've noticed at all Janice but I'm just the tiniest bit busy right now. I'm cooking you see, that's why I've got these funny clothes on.' Then this to his supplier: 'This is personal, I want to be rude. I am hoping to cause offence.' And Blackstock's depressing inability to make small talk with his diners: 'There are those that mingle and there are those that don't mingle. I belong to the latter category ... Je ne mingle pas.' How much he must have learned from watching workaholic John in the kitchen.

At home in front of the television, John watched and laughed, because he thought Lenny had him banged to rights. For once, the episodes actually made him laugh at himself although at the time of some of the stories, he was going through a difficult and had been taking life terribly seriously. However, seeing it in a hammed-up way and looking back at the stories he once thought so serious, he realised much of it had not actually been that way. The story of the missing blue plaster is a case in point. Having relayed the story to Tilbury, when John sat down and watched the episode on television, he half expected an irate restaurant manager to run in and say he had found someone's plaster in a dinner, just as John had told it. Instead, in the programme a commis chef slips on the kitchen floor, only to see the plaster under one of the hotplates. When it happened in real life, however, with all the tension that the plaster in the food had created, John had been going round the kitchen like a 'fucking madman', thinking he would never work again, only for Peter Tilbury to make a joke out of it. To a relieved John Burton-Race, it was fabulous.

23

CREATING A LEGACY

MARTIN BLUNOS entered the food industry for exactly the same reason as John: the simple love of cooking, which is a reflection of why John showed his friend the script for Chef! and sought his opinion. Martin's family was arty, his uncle having been quite a famous watercolour painter, and Martin's father said he should do something with food because people always have to eat, and cooking was an art. Once in the industry, however, it was not long before he realised that the higher up the ladder one went, the less time was actually spent in the kitchen. Suddenly, there are other people working for you while you are walking around with a clipboard and a phone pinned to your ear. 'Sometimes it is nice to jump in and do what you got into this business for in the first place,' he says. 'I tell my team in Bangkok, stay a commis chef or a junior for as long as you can. As long as you have enough money to pay the bills, you are going to amass this great wealth of experience. As soon as you start going up the ladder, instead of being shown what to do, you will be expected to show others.'

Martin and John went on to star in Taste The Nation, the popular British daytime cookery show hosted by Nick Hancock, with judges Henrietta Jane Green, William Sitwell and Richard Johnson. Representing Cornwall as chef captain, John made it through to the quarter finals, only to be defeated by Rosemary Shrager, representing Northumberland. Martin survived the first round before succumbing to the skills of County Down's Merrilees Parker. The eventual winner was Rosemary Shrager. John faired extremely well, heading up six chef's victories to Nick Nairn's leading score of seven, with Martin a solitary one with Graham Tinsley.

By this stage in his career, it had become clear to those in the know that John was a grafter. He was not living on his name alone and his food knowledge was second-to-none. Where other chefs may have achieved status in life by who they knew, John achieved his success the hard way — attending college and working his way through the ranks in some great kitchens — and when the media frenzy began, he was pretty much ready for anything. Martin came through that same learning curve. His own media frenzy began after a television appearance on the original MasterChef series, hosted by Lloyd Grossman. He and Sian were still living above Lettonie in Bristol at the time. Suddenly, cars were pulling up outside and people were peering through the windows; the power of media had struck. Television land is a flat panel. You can see it, but you can't smell it, taste it or touch it. Suddenly, the world wanted to smell, taste and touch Martin's food creations.

Another young chef making waves was a certain Michael Caines, who was very aware of the career path John had taken via the Blanc stable. He has vivid memories of John's skill at L'Ortolan and the fact that he had gained two Michelin stars in his own right. 'When you go to Le Manoir you are very aware of who has been before you and created a legacy for themselves,' he tells me. 'John achieved this through the achievement of others as well as for himself. A lot of people have worked for him and gone on in their own right; John having been one of the early ones, along with Marco Pierre White and others of that era.'

Caines was at Les Quat'Saisons for three years, having joined the team in the late 1980s as a commis chef and quickly progressing to sous chef. While John had long gone by this time, even during Caines' own time under Blanc, he recalls a number of British chefs looking up to people like John Burton-Race, realising that there was a path for themselves to follow. 'John has always been very much his own man and he had a reputation for it, both positive and negative. As an English chef, in those days there were not many two Michelin starred chefs so John's achievement was incredible, and although at the time he was very outspoken about the industry in terms of what he stood for and what he did, he was always talked in terms of his style of cooking.' Caines enjoyed his time as part of the Blanc stable but saw his career development coming from across the Channel. As a result, he headed to France for two years before returning and taking up station at Gidley Park in 1994. The holder of two Michelin stars for more than 18 years, he went to Lympstone Manor as chef and patron in 2016, where he was awarded a Michelin star just six months after opening.

In 1994, John and Nigel Marriage were offered a consultancy with British Airways and were duly charged with compiling menus for the company's transatlantic flights to New York on Concorde. BA, as a member of La Confrerie de la Chaine Rotisseurs—the world's oldest and most important gastronomical society, founded in 1248 and granted a Royal Charter in 1610—welcomed the privilege of continuing longstanding traditions of comfort, elegance and hospitality for the most discerning of travellers. The launch of the menus for the London-Anchorage-Tokyo-Osaka route was held at the Waldorf Astoria, where canapés were laced with Caviar Oscietra. It was opulence galore. John, who set his food by London standards, now found that New York had the edge. He was like a kid in a sweet shop, visiting Woodbury Common Premium Outlets, the ultimate destination for shopping and dining, where he browsed the multitude of high-end fashion retail brands, seeking out the cheaper end of designer clothing. He hit the department stores Century 21, Macy's and Bloomingdales but as always, food took centre stage. Mesmerized by the host of influential quarters, he found himself at the hub of a cosmopolitan gem and visited a steakhouse in Brooklyn called Lugeros. He had never seen such large portions of food before—trays of chips the size of tables and salads enough for five diners. He visited Daniels in the Upper East Side, an elegant French flagship restaurant where he had to wear a jacket and tout his expense account. At La Cirque, the iconic Midtown eatery, he enjoyed high-end French dining in a circus-themed setting. There were the delis and the Chinese quarter where he savoured Peking duck. On one evening he visited Robert de Niro's place in the docks. It was an hour before midnight as he ordered a crab salad and was amazed to see diners still filtering into the restaurant.

John and Nigel Marriage produced an exquisite menu for Concorde passengers.

Lunch

- Japanese delicacies with a selection of canapés.
- Golden Ascerta caviar presented in a wholemeal tartlet, accompanied by smoked sturgeon and a papilotte of smoked salmon and salmon mousse. Served with buttered brown bread.
- Chilled mango with a combination of citrus fruits.
- Hot hors d'oeuvre featuring a croustade of wild mushrooms and spears of asparagus soup.
- Chicken consommé garnished with pistachio quenelles.
- Chilled cream of mulligatawny soup.

Main Courses

- Roast rib eye of prime Scotch beef served with Yorkshire pudding and natural gravy.
- Grilled Dover soul and prawn dressed with herb butter and garnished with grilled vegetables.
- Braised breast of duckling with five spice sauce.
- A vegetarian speciality featuring a combination of fresh vegetables and nuts, baked in a case of light filo pastry and served with carrot sauce.
- Fresh leaf spinach, spring carrots, stuffed baby marrow, jetee promenade potatoes and rice pilaf.
- Selection of Japanese pickles.

Salad

- Mixed seasonal salad served with a choice of mustard vinaigrette or yoghurt and herb dressing.

Desserts

- A variety of fresh fruit and berries set in pink champagne.
- Creamy ice cream prepared from yoghurt and natural fruit purees.
- Basket of fresh seasonal fruits.

Cheese
- A fine selection of English cheeses including Stilton, Double Gloucester and Goats' cheese. Also recommended—Rougette, a new soft country cheese from Germany and Chavannes from France.

Coffee—Tea
- Coffee, decaffeinated coffee or tea served with a selection of fine chocolates.

Afternoon Tea
- Selection of sandwiches featuring chicken, prawns, egg with cress and salted brisket of beef.
- Light fruit scones served with strawberry preserve and clotted cream from the bakery.
- English tea cake and fresh fruit marignons.
- Choice of coffee or tea including Darjeeling, Earl Grey, Camomile.

Light Meal Appetizer
- Seafood salad. Served with turnip, soy and sesame vinaigrette

Light Main Courses
- Pan-fried entrecote steak garnished with a variety of wild mushrooms.
- Grilled fillet of fresh salmon dressed with parsley butter.

Vegetables
- French beans, stuffed courgettes, baby squash, Japanese rice and berry potatoes salad bowl.
- Mixed seasonal salad with tarragon vinaigrette or yoghurt, mustard and chive dressing.

Dessert
- Fresh fruit flan.
- Selection of cheeses, served with celery, crackers and butter.
- Variety of freshly prepared seasonal fruit.
- Coffee, decaffeinated coffee or tea.

After the success of Concorde, in 1995 John went on to win Cateys Chef of the Year. First held in 1984 when it was won by Michel Bourdin, The Cateys is a UK award ceremony for the hospitality industry, described as the equivalent of the Oscars, where recipients are nominated, selected and awarded by the industry through The Caterer magazine. The Chef Award is one of the most coveted, and John was to join a list of prestigious chefs which has included Claude Bosi, Angela Hartnett, Raymond Blanc and Tom Kerridge.

Spurred on by his success, John sat down to pen his first book. Published by Headline, John Burton-Race: Recipes From An English Master Chef contained an introduction by Egon Ronay, with a front cover image of a very young Mr Burton-Race and two of his creations. According to John, the book did not sell all that well. 'The photography was shit, the front cover was shit and it contained shit recipes. I look at it now and I think about all those people who write books or take photographs and reflect on their previous work and are so often embarrassed by it.' For the sake of curiosity and as part of my research, I found a copy on the internet. The sleeve mentions that John's career reached a peak at the 1992 Gastronomic Olympics in Madrid, where he competed against 14 cooks from other nations and picked up two gold medals and shared first place in the tournament. According to Michael Bateman in The Independent on Sunday, 'It was his originality, bravura and sheer skill that left the rest of Europe trailing.'

The book contains a series of practical, attentive recipes written according to the four seasons, with each quarter of the year detailing eight menus. At the back of the book is a section titled The Basics, which details how to make a variety of stocks, marinades, sauces, vinaigrettes, pastas and pastries. The book is certainly comprehensive.

In his introduction, Ronay wrote: 'I have known many chefs toiling obsessively, trying to make it, but unable to do so. I have known perfectionists who could dexterously give a tomato the faultless shape of a rose, but that pointless skill was their best. Others, amusing themselves at the stove, had intellect but lacked the gourmet's judgement. And I have seen cooks of gifted palates, with the divine spark of obsessive application. I have seen very, very few, in whom all these gifts culminate, as they do in John Burton-Race.' He went on to comment that John's rare gift of creating inexperienced tastes and flavours by instinctively bringing together ingredients in combinations that don't occur to anyone else, 'is what crowns him as one of the small handful of truly great chefs of England'.

John writes that a chef can only develop his or her own style once they are confident of their own ability. Seeking perfection in his craft since the age of 17, he admitted to being both pleased and proud that the majority of the restaurants and chefs he had encountered over the years had been French, resulting in food from his kitchen that was unashamedly influenced by classic French cuisine. In the acknowledgements, John wrote: 'Behind every kitchen lunatic there must be someone to stabilise and guide, to encourage and calm, and that person for me is my wife Christine. Without her I'd be lost.'

That statement came back to haunt John soon after, as the relationship with his long-standing and—he readily admits—long-suffering wife Marie-Christine began to crack, and the marriage fell apart. She eventually burnt out, which John attributes to a combination of both himself and the business, which saw him putting in endless days and late nights in the kitchen at L'Ortolan. The couple was also late in having children, as John had shown little interest during their time together, being far too ambitious to worry about offspring. It was not until he was in his 30s that Naomi and Max were born. He loves them dearly and the break-up occurred when Max was very young and Naomi at the tender age of 12; a time in their lives when having a father figure was important. It was almost as if he was seeing his own childhood mirrored before him.

John and Marie-Christine separated after 17 years together. During the last three years of their marriage, John tells me Marie-Christine had been in and out of an alcohol dependency clinic. He remembers being asleep one night when at about two in the morning, he woke up to find her 'beating the shit' out of him. 'It was quite disconcerting, and I was terrified, so I moved out the bedroom. There was no sex for years and I just didn't want her anywhere near me. I was doing consultancy work in Mauritius and would take her with me for a holiday, when she would disgrace herself and embarrass me. I admit to feeling some element of guilt because I thought part of her cracking up had been due to me and another part had been the job, and the pressure that brought with it. To be honest, it doesn't matter now. When a person is not well and they have something going on inside their head, another person cannot either see or imagine that illness. I always carried around some of the pressure of myself, and I am sure that helped make her like she was. I have always carried that guilt. It wasn't my fault but I certainly didn't help because I was always 100 per cent, 16 hours a day full on about the business and nothing else but the business, allied to the high standards I was constantly striving to maintain.' John relied on his wife to play her part in the business and when she finally went, he realised he had lost something vital. Marie-Christine eventually took the children to live in France and it was not until some years later that John saw his son again, quite by chance, at Naomi's wedding, when she asked her father to give her away. Max said he had been studying psychology at the University of Tours in America. 'Perhaps he could work on me, and help me out,' was John's immediate thought.

I spoke to Naomi from her home in Paris. 'At the time of my parents' separation I had idea what was going on. I was heartbroken at not having my dad around and put the blame on my mum and was terribly badly behaved with her at that point,' she says. 'I now realise she was the bravest and the most loving and supporting mummy I could ever wish for, and she dealt with the situation in the best possible way to preserve my brother and I.' Today, Naomi works for Airbus Defence and Space as Head of External Communications and Media Relations, with responsibility for the company's image on an international scale. Max is a psychologist and works at a retirement complex, dealing with pensioners and their families. He resides in Bourges on the Yèvre river in central France.

'At the beginning I saw my father a few times. He took me to the park and an indoor playground. I don't recall Max being there. He was three at the time,' says Naomi. 'That was the first year. Then we only saw Dad for a few minutes at a time, twice a year for my birthday and Christmas. He would pull up in front of our house in a smart car that stood out in the neighbourhood we were in and brought us gifts. We would stay together on the front lawn or in his car and then he would leave. Sometimes, if I was lucky, we would drive around the neighbourhood together in his car. That happened for perhaps two years until he stopped coming. The young girl that I was didn't really have an explanation as to why, but all I know is that the next two or three visits — the last ones—were made by L'Ortolan's gardener. That's who my mum told me it was when he came. The presents stopped shortly after, as did the visits and communication between Dad and me. It brutally ceased and stayed that way for about 12 years. Max doesn't recall much and didn't see Dad a lot either. He didn't come to the playground with us and he met his father for the first time since the divorce, as far as he can remember, at my wedding in October 2017.'

John met his second wife Kim in 1996 on a Caribbean island they both happened to be visiting for a mutual friend's birthday. At the time they were both married, and John was there with Marie-Christine and their children. Kim was a friend of the bridegroom and dined at L'Ortolan at least once a week, and they both worked in the travel industry. With his marriage in tatters, the last thing John was looking for was another relationship as his work continued to take precedence, but seeing Kim at the airport, he was hooked, lined and sinkered. 'I hadn't done any of the running. I was run after,' he tells me. 'I loved the whole attention thing.'

While John's marriage floundered, his business was a success and he was being talked about in all the right circles. Perhaps it was time once again for the release valve to blow and bugger the consequences. Raymond Blanc had once told Gary Jones that to work in a kitchen, you needed to have a frontal lobotomy, with no brain left to work in that environment. Back in the day, there was little wonder that parents were often fearful of sending their children into such chaotic environments, where only the mad would survive. On the other hand, those same children needed to work alongside the likes of the John Burton-Races, Marco Pierre Whites and Pierre Koffmans of this crazy world, because they were the standard bearers. If you wanted to get on, you needed to get yourself alongside them. In life you have to be accountable for everything you say and do, and when John was cooking at his prime, it was nothing short of phenomenal and he was possibly second-to-none in the country. It was not just about the quality of the food being produced either, but the quality of the experience of the people in the kitchen, as well as the service team. It is impossible to succeed one without the other. But niceties have not always followed suit; his motto was to crack on with it and survive the day. And he knew in his heart that having been exposed to the brutality of kitchen life, there was only one way to go for the industry—to make sure the environment was the best it could possibly be, so when new people came in, they knew it was the right place for them.

When chefs are performing at the highest level every night, the natural tendency is to aspire to make every plate perfect, but more often than not chef will invariably think it could be bettered. In this respect, John is no different to any other chef. That is the professionalism in all of them, and even though staff may experience a tough night, it is often the customer who puts it in perspective. Even so, the John Burton-Races of this world continued to beat themselves up about it, as no doubt did the likes of Marco Pierre White and Bernard Loiseau, who sadly is not with us anymore, having tragically taken his own life. What Michael Caines learnt from Loiseau was that knowing the customer had a good night, no matter how bad his might have been in the kitchen, made him feel better.

Things are totally different today, with social media and websites like TripAdviser where the public freely post what they like, when they like, regardless of the repercussions to the individual or their restaurant. Today's chef, therefore, must be far more careful of what he says rather than what he does, because so many things can be amplified out of both context and proportion. The wiser man will say nothing or be conservative about what is said. Even then, because that wiser chef is in the public eye, it can draw sensational headlines and sensationalism. The aspiring chef can never really relax, because they will have one eye on what they do and the other on what people think. No wonder it continues to be such a crazy industry.

As John was collecting his Cateys Award in 1995, the year also saw him betrothed to Kim. They went on to have two children together, Charles and Amelia. He had more or less fallen into the relationship when he was at an all-time low. He had been dealing with a nanny who was, in his own words, a bitch, and Marie-Christine had spent the latter part of their marriage in and out of rehab. Like many a young man, no doubt he had thought about sex before engaging his brain.

24

DISAPPEARING ACT

In 1998, living in Shipton-on-Stour in Warwickshire, Dennis Race was diagnosed with myeloma. He died in the July while undergoing treatment. 'Dad had an immense pain threshold,' says Rebecca. 'I remember once when he underwent root canal treatment without anaesthetic. His death was a knock for all of us. Mum was really low for 12 years. I didn't think she would pull herself out of it, but she was quite a strong character. She got involved in various groups, such as the bridge club and the choir, and met a teacher called Paddy. He was a very bright man but with no common sense whatsoever. He had never married and had been the main carer for his parents. After buying a bungalow together in Shropshire, Paddy and Mum lived together for a while as companions before they eventually married. Sadly, Paddy was diagnosed with bowel cancer and died in 2009. My then husband Chris and I decided that we would buy a house and have an annex erected so Mum could live with us, while being of independent means. She spent a lot of time looking after my son George when he was a toddler and had a massive impact on him.' Diagnosed with lung cancer, Shirley died in 2014.

In 1999, Jamie upped sticks and left L'Ortolan. While not particularly bright academically, he had shown an interest in cookery, but it was becoming evident to John that he was itching to take his life in a different direction—anywhere, in fact, other than under his stepbrother's feet. After Dennis Race's death, Shirley offered to treat her children to a wonderful holiday to remember him by. Shirley and her daughter Rebecca were talking about an adventure in the Galapagos Islands. Jamie had Thailand in his sights so off he went on a solo ten-day trip, happily bouncing back into Heathrow Airport carrying Shirley's credit card, which she had given him in case he needed money in an emergency. What did he do next? He bought a first-class ticket back to Thailand. That was it—no conversation with the family. Gone. The next the family heard from him was a short time later when he contacted John saying he had had an accident and was in hospital. He required surgery and asked John to wire him money. John immediately contacted Rebecca, today an A&E consultant, who in turn contacted the hospital—only to discover it was a lie.

With contacts at the prestigious Raffles hotel in Thailand where John had been acting in a consultancy capacity, he managed to swing Jamie a job in the kitchen as a chef, but he never turned up and went AWOL. I ask John to elaborate on the time leading up to Jamie's disappearance in the Far East, and his comments are tinged with both sadness and resignation. Dennis Race had given his adopted son more than £30,000, secured a mortgage for him on a two-up, two-down house on a small estate close to Le Manoir, and bought him a car so he could commute to work. While Jamie was doing all right for himself in the kitchen, Raymond Blanc had been under the impression that he would never make a brilliant chef. He had, however, proven himself to be a dutiful and hard worker. With Jamie's sudden disappearance, John tried, albeit unsuccessfully, to take over the mortgage payments so at least he would have a home to come back to, should Jamie ever decide to return. Unfortunately, the property was repossessed and sold at auction and the deposit was lost. It was then left up to John to sell the car.

Over the course of the next five years, Jamie phoned John perhaps only three times. Eventually having told his brother where he was living, John and Kim flew to Thailand. Jamie had initially told them not to bother but the day after their arrival, he turned up at their hotel and explained he had fallen in love with a local girl from a bar when he had been on holiday, and she became pregnant. A heated discussion ensued between the brothers, and it transpired that Jamie had only been seeing the girl for two weeks. Jamie was so scared about the situation that he hadn't dared return to England to tell his mother. John saw through the scam and told him his so-called girlfriend had deliberately picked him up, Jamie admitted that she had cleaned him out. He had been giving her money and she had then been running down the street and passing it on to her pimp. Jamie then got involved in a fight with the pimp because he was behind with a payment, and as a result had to leave the area because his cronies threatened to kill him.

The following day Jamie visited John again. It was a hot and sultry morning, and John suggested they go for a swim to cool off. Jamie, however, refused to roll his sleeves up, let alone take his top off. Instead, he mounted a moped and rode away. The next morning, while John was having breakfast, Jamie turned up again and admitted to self-harming. He then explained that he was working at a five-star resort down the coast. When John went to check, he found out that Jamie had been sacked because a bunch of people had come after him, no doubt after money again. He'd moved to a place called Buffalo Bills, a grill for tourists at Hua Hin, a seaside resort on the Gulf of Thailand Buffalo Bills was run by a man from Essex who immediately began to slag Jamie off—until John actually told him who he was. Deciding there was little chance of catching up with his stepbrother, John suddenly caught sight of him on his moped with a teenage girl on pillion. Apparently, she was just a friend. John asked why everything was so complicated and Jamie replied that he wouldn't understand. He then admitted that had been feeding himself on the equivalent of £1.40 a day, obtaining food and drink from street sellers, and had no money to speak of. With plans to return to the UK via Bangkok the next day, John told him to come to the hotel. John convinced Kim they should give him $1,000US—and that was the last he ever saw or heard from him.

'I don't know where he is or whether he is still alive,' says John. 'I tried to track him down again. I didn't want him working at some shitty place in the back end of Thailand. In a way I don't really blame him for wanting to lead his own life. I am just conscious that if we had left it another two weeks, he would be dead. My mother, although in a way she did a wonderful thing by adopting him, her methods were a bit crazy. Psychiatrists had told her that Jamie would never come to anything in his life. He was very quiet and would never speak to anyone, so there were clearly personality defects which possibly had been caused by malnutrition during the first 14 months of his life, although to all intents and purposes, looking at him as an adult you would never know. To this day, I don't know why my parents took on this hopeless toddler, but my mother used up lots of energy to try and make something of him. Typically, she assumed that with the lifestyle she could offer and all the money, she could make him into something, but he simply had no ambition. He didn't really want money, although he was always given it. Certainly, my parents gave him a better head start than I ever had, financially and in every other way, but he didn't give a shit. He didn't really want any of it. In a way, he probably had to get away from being shaped into something he never would be or wanted to be.'

25

TAKING STOCK

B Y THE year 2000, after more than 14 years at L'Ortolan, John took
stock of his life. On the one hand he had become attached to the
place, in part because it was his first solo venture and he had managed
to turn it round, but it had proved a long and painful road. On the flipside,
throughout his life he had lived a bohemian existence, a nomad flitting from
country to country, school to school, from one kitchen to the next, never
forging great bonds with anyone, simply because the opportunity had never
presented itself. In typical Burton-Race fashion and leaving aside his youth, at
no point did he actually start to feel sorry for himself because he had enjoyed
every moment of his culinary journey. At L'Ortolan, he had reached an impasse.
He began to wonder how far he could take it, with two Michelin stars already
in the bag and the cash tills ringing the same old tune. Basically, he needed
money and ended selling a parcel of land attached to the property. Having
secured the sum of £350,000, he brought the restaurant back in the black and
decided to sell. Gratefully accepting the money, he then proceeded to blow it
all in London in search of the bright lights and his next culinary adventure.

'I loved my time at L'Ortolan,' he tells me. 'It was a way of life for all those years, and there were certainly some ups in my career. First a Michelin star in my first year, then a second in year two, followed by Restaurant of the Year, European Chef of the Year, Cateys Chef of the Year, winner of the Chambre Syndicate and Haute Cuisine Francais in Madrid, to name but a few. But it had not always been rosy. Finances had always been an issue and my personal life was a mess. However, I can look back with gratitude because it was the first place where I could realise my ambitions and in the main it was very rewarding.'

One of the favourite dishes on the Sunday lunch menu with diners was sea bass for two, prepared to a classic French recipe. The technique also works with other fish such as sea bream and by slightly changing the ingredients, it can also work for leg of new season lamb or rack of lamb.

SEA BASS IN SALT
(Serves 2)

Ingredients
1.5kg cleaned fish, not scaled
Handful of fennel tops or dill
2 sprigs fresh thyme
6 egg whites
175g salt

Method
1. Pre-heat the oven to 200 °C.
2. Put the fennel tops or dill and sprigs of thyme into the cavity of the sea bass.
3. Whisk the egg whites in a mixture. Simply break them up a little and as soon as they appear like a soft peak (frothy), add the salt.
4. Once the salt is fully incorporated, remove from the mixer and allow to rest in the refrigerator for about an hour.
5. In a large oval ovenproof dish just large enough to accommodate

the fish, put a thin layer of salt on the bottom. Lay the fish on top and then completely cover the fish in a thick layer of salt.

6. Spray a little water over the fish and bake for about 40 minutes. The salt will act like a hard, airtight brick.

Serve this with a tomato buerre blanc, flavoured with anchovies.

A tomato fondue works for this dish, and one of John's favourite dishes is Artichokes Barigoule.

TOMATO FONDUE

Ingredients
4 beef tomatoes
150ml olive oil
Zest of a lemon
2 cloves garlic (peeled)
Salt
Juice of half a lemon
3 sprigs lemon thyme
Milled black pepper
1tsp sugar

Method
1. Preheat the oven to 400°C.
2. Cut the tomatoes cross-wise and squeeze out the seeds.
3. Line a baking tray with a sheet of parchment paper and place the tomato halves cut side down on the paper and bake in the oven for about 10 minutes.
4. Peel off the tomato skins and transfer the flesh to a saucepan with all the remaining ingredients.
5. Cook over a gentle heat for at least two hours or until most of the liquid has evaporated.
6. Remove the sprigs of lemon thyme and transfer the fondue to a small bowl.

ARTICHOKE BARIGOULE

Ingredients

1 tbsp lemon juice
6 baby artichokes
2 tbsp olive oil
2 cloves garlic
Large pinch of salt
1 glass white wine
1 sprig fresh thyme
1 sprig rosemary

Method

1. In a large bowl, add a pint of water and the lemon juice.
2. Cut off the tops of the artichokes and remove the outer leaves. Trim with a sharp knife or peeler (turn).
3. Quarter the turned artichokes lengthways and put them in the water quickly.
4. Heat 1 tablespoon of olive oil in a saucepan over a medium heat.
5. Drain the water from the artichokes. Put them into the oil and add the garlic. Sauté for about 2 minutes, then season with salt and pepper.
6. Add the wine and bring the pan to the boil. Add the remaining olive oil, thyme and rosemary. Cover the pan.
7. Continue to cook over a medium heat until the artichokes are tender. This will take about 4 minutes.
8. Pour the artichokes into a bowl and reserve aside for the other seasonings and ingredients.

VEGETABLES AND SEASONINGS

Ingredients

100g blanched, skinned broad beans

50g diced taggiasca olives

1 blanched, diced red pepper

Black milled pepper

Method

Mix all the above and sprinkle all of the above ingredients over the artichokes.

26

FRENCH LEAVE

During his tenure at L'Ortolan, John grew it into one of the most prestigious restaurants in the UK, alongside Le Manoir Aux Quat'Saisons, The Waterside Inn and Le Gavroche. The restaurant was purchased by IT entrepreneur Peter Newman, who appointed Alan Murchison as head chef.

Like many things in life, John thought he had grown attached to the place, but realistically, having lived much his life in a semi-nomadic way from childhood, he never forged great bonds with anyone, anything or any place. In 2000, with several hundred thousand pounds in his bank account, his eyes fixated on London for his next culinary adventure.

'John is a deeply troubled man,' Michael Caines believes. 'I have had many a chat with him and it goes back to his childhood, and I know that haunts him and quite heavily affects him to this today. Yes, he is resilient, but he gets himself into some crazy situations that only a person such as John could get himself into. He makes some situations difficult for himself, because when the subject matter may be controversial or he loses focus, he behaves in a particular way which people find difficult to stomach, and he is a bit out there. Deep down though, there is a very thoughtful and considerate person well aware of some of the issues that surround him, and he is very resilient.'

In a case like that of John Burton-Race, you can go off the radar, but you cannot disappear forever. When I explained to people that I was gathering material for his biography, some looked at me quizzically. They most certainly know the name, but it is only when I show them a photograph that realisation dawns. 'Wasn't he the one who had all those children in France and then left his wife for another woman?' Scandal always seems to come before the culinary brilliance. During certain periods in his career, John has struggled to find the right opportunity to put himself back where he belongs — in the kitchen. Never mind all that nonsense about the modern executive chef so prevalent in today's world, stalking the kitchens with clipboard to hand, ordering food, hiring and firing staff, and admin, admin, admin, wearing chef's whites but never picking up a dishcloth or kitchen knife. John cannot control what people think of him, but he can cook great food for people to enjoy. Despite all of the ups and downs, he continues to persevere in doing what he loves best.

While John had achieved critical acclaim at his provincial restaurant with its two Michelin stars and five AA rosettes, he was conscious that a London site would hopefully bring him closer to his client base and, ultimately, give him a steadier source of revenue. Having put the word out, it was not long before the owners of London's Landmark Hotel on Marylebone Road asked their representative, Brian Cladnick, to seek him out. At the time, the Thai owners also had the K Club in Shepherd's Bush and the Landmark Bangkok. John was informed that there was space available for a new restaurant in London, so he took the opportunity and sank his money into the enterprise, building a state-of-the-art kitchen, while Kim handled the design of the restaurant. Having set about hiring staff, the penny soon dropped that he would have to pay double for anyone working in London compared to the countryside. He ploughed on and it was certainly worthwhile, because by year one he gained his second Michelin star back, scored five for The Most Comfortable Dining Room in London ... and then proceeded to go broke due to overheads.

John initially signed a five-year lease but come 2002 and the start of the third financial year, he knew he wouldn't afford the monthly rent. The owners, however, very much liking what they were seeing, told him they were happy to defer the payments. Once again with his mind in turmoil, not knowing which way to go for the best, when he was offered a lifeline—an opportunity for him and the family to head to France for a year, accompanied by a film crew for a proposed television series. It was quite by chance that one of his regular customers came to the rescue. Steve Smith, who worked in television and was the manager of the Graham Norton show, would often turn up late in the evening for dinner with his partner. Steve would ask John what he could cook, and he always obliged, despite numerous 2am finishes and 6am starts. John was living in Chiswick at the time and although he was on the fringes of central London and not too far from the restaurant, the daily grind was beginning to impact on his health. He would happily tell Steve and his partner about his dreams and aspirations, and in particular his love of France. One evening, Smith told John that he would like him to meet Pat Llewellyn, who ran a production company called Optimum Television. Pat was the producer who discovered the Two Fat Ladies and Jamie Oliver and was the founder of Naked Chef. Although John had never heard of her, and there was no reason why he should have, Pat proved instrumental in his next move. The head of Channel 4 at the time had been trying to get Pat to work with Gordon Ramsay but apparently, she had taken a dislike to him, although she did eventually work with the outspoken chef. According to John, Smith booked Pat in for dinner, explaining that it would be a table for three … and on the night in question only Pat turned up. John received a call to say the boys couldn't make it, so he would have to look after his guest on his own. Pat was understandably put out at first, until John said he would dine with her, and even better, she didn't have to pay. Pat's response was to ask why he would do that, as he didn't even know her, and John replied that she could be a guinea pig for a few dishes he wasn't sure about. The couple began eating and talking, and John explained how he longed to return to France to get back on the stove and to start learning about cooking all over again.

Pat returned a week later to say she had someone interested in him appearing in a television series, and the following week she asked whether he and his family could move to France the very next day. According to John, Pat had been intrigued by the fact he had never actually cooked for his children, and dispatching the family off to France would provide him with that opportunity; the idea of the television series being to show John in a natural environment, a sort of how-to-change-your-life show, with food in the mix.

A book deal was also in the offering, and John soon found himself sitting down with several agents. He wanted to go with Penguin because he thought the representatives were young and hip, but then a woman came in from Ebury, bringing with her a picnic basket filled with foie gras and cheeses. Penguin clearly didn't like it. While the negotiating process was supposed to involve sealed bids, Penguin knew they had outbid their rivals. Ebury, however, won the contract, and John landed himself a record advance of £350,000 plus a ghostwriter to relay his story about his life in France. The book was translated into French and realised sales in 13 countries and provided him with royalties for the next decade. That year away also helped get his sanity back on track.

John accepted the commission from Channel 4 realising that his marriage was floundering. While it had been good for the first four years, in 2002 he realised there was a problem. But his immediate focus was on keeping John Burton-Race at The Landmark and funding it by dropping his salary and maintain the outgoings through monies he would earn from the television series, which was to be entitled French Leave. It sounded simple but then things are never simple with John Burton-Race. The moment he left London, the restaurant began to lose three times as much money as it had done in its first two years, partly because he wasn't there but also because of the people he had trusted to run the business in his absence. Let's just say there was a great deal of no sales. Part-way through filming, he flew back from France and told the owners they could take him to court for the last two years of the lease because he had already decided to tell the staff that their services were no longer required. Then he promptly flew back to France. The owners, to their credit, told John that because he had given them something special, and even though his tenure had been short-lived, they had the cachet of owning the only two-star Michelin hotel in the whole of London and he had been very honourable about the whole affair. He had built a new kitchen, which they would take, thank you very much, and the restaurant looked fabulous, so they were happy. As for John, he walked away from the venture a little bit like one of his marriages, without a penny except for the pants he was wearing. After fourteen-and-a-half years of battling and £850,000 lighter, he left it to them.

On January 16, 2003, Amanda Afiya reported in Caterer & Hotelkeeper magazine that after months of speculation, the London Landmark hotel confirmed its flagship restaurant, John Burton-Race at the Landmark, had closed at the end of 2002 and that John, who was in France filming his forthcoming television programme for Channel 4, was unavailable for comment. A spokesman for the hotel said the chef had opened the 70-seat restaurant on May 23, 2000, having signed an agreement to rent the space from the hotel for five years, but was now concentrating on other activities. According to the report, sources suggested the restaurant had a poor financial record. In August, Burton-Race told *Caterer* that the restaurant had suffered particularly badly following the events of September 11. 'I've never seen such an exodus from London,' said John at the time. 'I personally lost £86,000 of business in holiday cancellations.' However, he added that he felt that 'things were looking better'. The Landmark said it had no plans for the space occupied by Burton-Race, although it added that it would probably be used as an additional banqueting room in the short term.

27

COBBLERS COVE

IT WAS perhaps fortunate that while at The Landmark, John earned an extra income through consultancy work, with one location being the idyllic Cobblers Cove, the only Relais & Chateaux hotel in Barbados. Situated on the west coast and one of the Caribbean's best-known luxury hotels, the resort combines the elegance and charm of an English country house hotel with the tropical style and luxurious gardens of Barbados.

'I had been going there for about 15 years and I love the place,' John tells me. 'It is an absolute gem, very old-fashioned and hasn't changed for years. Although it has been freshened up, I am sure it is just the same as when it was a private house, being very small, very intimate, personal and fabulous.'

Upon arrival at Cobblers Cove, guests are greeted with a stunning welcome as they catch sight of the sun-washed coral pink stone frontage of the Great House overlooking the blue waters of the ocean beyond. The house is home to the multi award-winning Camelot Restaurant and Bar, open to balmy tropical breezes and overlooking the palm-fringed beach and poolside deck. Despite modern amenities there is much at Cobblers Cove that reflects its

Bajan heritage, and the restaurant's menu is heavy with local delicacies. During John's time there, the courtly Scottish-educated general manager Hamish Watson placed emphasis on casual outdoor living in a country house atmosphere, complete with a pleasant combination of British reserve and easy-going Bajan friendliness. Watson, whose Caribbean roots go back seven generations, set a tone that was neither too formal nor too loose. Restaurant diners were not required to wear jacket and tie, though high jinks around the pool were frowned upon. Centrepiece of a stay at Cobblers Cove was the superb food, where the hotel's cooks were adept at blending British culinary discipline with island flair, the accent being on fresh seafood. Specialties included tuna tartare with capers and hoisin sauce, grilled barracuda with Bajan seasoning and sea bass baked with morels. A favourite with diners was blackened flying fish served with a spiced pear chutney and pink peppercorn vinaigrette, while the wine list leant toward New World offerings, primarily from Argentina, Australia, New Zealand, South Africa, Chile and California.

Cobblers Cove held a four-day culinary festival in November 2002 featuring some of John's specialties. The new executive chef at the time, Mike Taylor, had been a Burton-Race protégé for the previous eight years. John had actually appointed two consultant chefs there during his own consultancy, and while it all sounded wonderful, things did not always go to plan. While working at one of the Caribbean food festivals, he recalls a particularly bad night. 'You know what chefs are like. I think they are all the same, it's not just me,' John says. 'They get grumpy because they take everything so personally. Their food must be exactly as they envisaged it. It could be that they are bad teachers so they can't get their team to work with them and get exactly what they want. It could be that the image in their mind never quite reaches the expectation, or that expectation never reaches reality. Anyway, the following morning after one really bad service I walked in, and there used to be a big mamma of a girl who was a lovely character and she used to take care of the breakfast service. She made the most delicious banana bread and I've still got the recipe. Everyone was trying to get rid of this woman because she was a bit old school. We were trying to move the food on, trying to make changes, and she wasn't having any of it. She had a one-track trained mind to do a job her way and that was how it had to be done. But I liked her nevertheless, because she was a real character. That morning I was grumpy and saying such things as, "Come on what are we doing here? You shouldn't have done this, and you shouldn't have done that," and she said, "Man you gotta chill out chef, you gonna go mad. What you need is a woman, a bottle of rum and a beach and go an' enjoy yourself". When I replied that I had no woman, I had no rum and I did not have time to go to the beach unless she wanted to come with me, she told me I was not her type. That was the kind of character she was and looking back now she was an essential part of the team really. If nothing else, she was someone to moan about.'

During John's time in Barbados he learnt about local fish, including wahoom dorado, kingfish and flying fish. While at Mullins Bay he saw a particularly famous dish using flying fish named Couteau de Pecheur—a toasted fish sandwich served with a fresh salad and rich mayonnaise with small deep-fried fillets of flying fish dipped in flour and Cajun spices. John sat there enjoying a cold Banks beer on a beach looking out over a turquoise sea, with the sun and a warm breeze on his face. 'I don't know whether that's a food memory or because it was so beautiful, or both, but the thing is when you are talking about food memories you usually associate them with a time and a place, one usually of pleasure, and I think that's why it goes hand in hand.'

That experience prompted him to prepare a special dish on a barbecue by the swimming pool every Friday evening. He would marinate wahoom, which is similar to king mackerel, in a touch of soya sauce, grated fresh ginger, garlic and lemon grass, parcelled in banana leaves and grilled on a very low heat. Bringing it to the table and opening up the leaf to release the smell of wonderful Asian spices, the fish dripping and making its own juice, there is little wonder those Friday evenings were a magical experience for diners.

The mention of banana leaves prompts John to tell me how as a child in the Far East, he soon discovered there were dozens of different types of the fruit. His favourite is called Pisang Suu, Pisang being the Malaysian word for banana and susu for milk. The bananas are no more than two or three inches long and an inch wide and are akin to having a concentrated sugary banana flavour with rich clotted cream. John would enjoy one with a slice of papaya squeezed with lime for his breakfast.

Cobblers Cove is also home to the notorious Cobblers Cooler, a volcanic blend of exotic fruit juices and countless Barbadian rums served in an oversized goblet. It is the basis for the infamous Cobblers challenge: any guest who can drink five servings of the lethal concoctions in one sitting, walk entirely around the white edge of the swimming pool without pausing or falling in, wins a week's stay at the hotel. There is a catch — if anyone looks likely to win, the manager reserves the right to mix the final cocktail himself. According to Hamish Watson, during his tenure at Cobblers only one guest successfully completed the challenge and needed the extra week to recuperate. He did not emerge from his room for two full days.

28

RED WINE AND A
TIMELY ENEMA

HAVING BEGUN his apprenticeship in London, before running his own restaurant, John never really warmed to the heady mix of city life. As far as he was concerned, those early days had a profound effect on him, working with kitchen staff who were permanently coked out of their heads and others not even able to stand up because they had so much white powder hanging out of their noses. He would always joke about being on his own natural high, driven by his work and excited about what he was cooking. He often had trouble with some of his boys in places he either owned or worked at, because they often had a drink or coke habit. They would tell him they couldn't do a particular task without a fix. Asking what they meant, they would tell him they were not addicts but on a Saturday night it would get them 'buzzing'. John's response was to tell them that he got his buzz when he was 'totally in the shit'. 'I would not let them start cooking until I knew we were fucked, because I always think you cook better under pressure, and they would get really upset,' he tells me. Some chefs had stormed out of his kitchen because he had done it too often, but when he could see all the checks lined up on the board, he would simply fight through as fast as he could and not take any prisoners because adrenalin would cut through him like a knife. You could not speak to him, because one tap on the shoulder would start him screaming. He was in the zone. People would then say that he was a madman — and maybe a part of him was.

A typical example was at the start of 2019 when John gained some consultancy work in Vietnam. Suddenly he was doing 100 covers in a country he had never cooked in before. Not knowing who he was working with or the kitchen he was working in, he was given less than 48 hours to prepare for 100 people over seven courses. That's 700 plates of food with a new team and no one understanding a word he was saying, apart from the two executive chefs. John was running over to one department, tasting sauces, before jumping in on an hors d'ouevre, helping the team dress the plate to his exacting requirements. They were looking at him as if he was mad, and he was very conscious of that. If only he could just be the chef cooking and not have an argument because someone stuck their thumb in his sauce, and not have to worry about how many people were round that table. He found himself working more or less as a chef de partie, doing as much of the cooking as he could and getting on with the job in hand, with the elder of the two executive chefs running out of steam in the first 20 minutes of service. A lovely bloke, according to John, but he couldn't manage the pressure. John was happy to remove himself from any hostility in the kitchen, so when the exec chef lost the plot and started shouting, John simply laughed. It was a long time since he had done that.

Life had not been without humour at John Burton-Race at The Landmark. On one particular evening, the sommelier showed a customer the label of the bottle of red wine he had ordered, pulled the cork, smelled the cork, poured the wine and walked away. The diner then reached into the top pocket of his suit and pulled out a small thermometer. He placed it in his glass of rather fine wine and promptly called the sommelier back to the table, complaining haughtily, 'This wine should be a maximum of eleven degrees, and it is twelve-and-a-half. Tell Mr. Burton-Race I am not paying for this wine.' The sommelier called over the restaurant manager and they went into a huddle. Having explained the situation to John, he asked if the diner was correct about the £90 bottle of wine, it being a mere one-and-a half degrees over. John fetched a large thermometer from the kitchen and told his sommelier to go back out to the customer and say that Mr. Burton-Race was coming to shove it up his arse, to gauge what temperature he was blowing shit out at. But no, thought John, that would never do. Not wanting to place any further pressure on his sommelier, John did the next best thing. He went into the restaurant and said to the diner, 'I understand there is something wrong with your wine. If you would you like to bend over the table while I shove this up your arse, I can then see what temperature you are running at.' 'It was like John Cleese on steroids,' he recalls. 'I didn't laugh. In fact, I was really angry, and I said, "By the way, I am not cooking for you, and there is no charge. That wine is beautiful, and when you have left the restaurant I will sit down and have dinner, and I will drink it. You can fuck off". I forgot myself completely. That's why I never get called out to the restaurant when it's too much, because I would just lose it.'

John is fully aware of the fact that the more chefs are talked about and the more accolades they get, the more they attract a certain type, which is fine because that is to be expected. Like everything in life, you take the rough with the smooth. But when it becomes completely unreasonable or intolerable, John Burton-Race often reacted, and with gusto. 'I am not the most politically correct of people. However bad the Press said Marco Pierre White, Paul Hollihead, Nigel Marriage, myself and other individuals were, I am not saying it was correct or right or true, but however bad we were, we were definitely a lot less bad than where we came from when we were doing our apprenticeships.'

Running John Burton-Race at The Landmark, he would rise in the early hours before anyone else in the household stirred, drive to London, and return home at gone 1am, day in, day out. He was on a conveyor belt he was struggling to get off, until that golden egg of an opportunity arose for him to spend some precious time in France. Even at L'Ortolan while in his early 30s he experienced heart problems because of his work ethic. Sleeping a maximum of three hours a night, occasionally only two, he was in danger of burnout. Driven by adrenalin, he only had himself to blame if things went badly wrong with his health. Chain-smoking and drinking, he told his doctor he could not remember when he'd last had a proper meal, and that caffeine kept him going. 'When you are younger you are motivated by your own ego and ambition, and then when you are older you are conscious of having to earn enough money for school fees and household bills,' he says. 'Then you get a colossal wipeout with a divorce and you go down. Then there are the character assassinations. I can name you any number of well-known chefs, household names, with lifestyles similar to mine who never had any of that, so how come I got it?' He has a point.

29

KING OF CASSOULET

JOHN HAD been in France six months before the family joined him properly. He found a delightful if ramshackle farmhouse in the tiny hamlet of Montferrand, deep in the Aude countryside, a département of the region of Languedoc Roussillon in southwest France. John tells me it was a last-minute choice after a frustrating period of house hunting. He soon found himself in his element. With no staff to worry about or bills to pay, everything felt right. However, those years of early mornings and late nights in London and before that in Berkshire had seen him in a routine which he found impossible to break, and because of that, he was still leaving the farmhouse at 7am and not returning until the early hours of the following morning, when he would chat and drink copious amounts of wine with the television crew. Those early mornings saw him busying himself at markets where he was surrounded by local, fresh produce. One of his favourite markets was in the 14th century town of Revel, where he loved the brightly canopied stalls outside the covered areas. It was everything he had come to expect from France, with its throngs of people, stalls piled high with food, and a wonderful atmosphere. He thought about the market all the way home after his first visit. 'Seeing those wonderful ingredients made me excited about food all over again, and I wanted to learn exactly why they were so fantastic,' he wrote in French Leave. While he was desperate to speak with local producers, he struggled to understanding the dialect, which is derived from the medieval language, langue 'd'Oc. At first, he managed to get by on smiles and sign language and a spattering of French.

John was well aware of the many different dishes that passed into folklore in different regions of France. The speciality in southwestern France, for example, is cassoulet, a rich, slow-cooked casserole containing white beans, duck fat and pork. The dish is named after its traditional cooking vessel, the cassole, a deep, round, glazed terracotta bowl with slanting sides. 'Cassoulet is big business here,' he wrote, 'not only because it is served in virtually every restaurant in the region but because it's France's main tinned food: at least six varieties of the stuff are sold in any good local supermarket'.

The word cassoulet was almost to prove John's undoing as a celebrity chef in the area, as one winter's evening while enjoying supper at a friend's house with Kim and with the subject naturally turning to food, John was told that if he really wanted to be taken seriously by people in the food business, he would have to become a member of the Grande Confrérie du Cassoulet. Slightly worse for wear after too much wonderful French wine, he asked what was involved. The answer: to make a good cassoulet, nothing more. It sounded simple enough, until he had sobered up the next day and realised what a monumental task he had agreed to. For starters, the food would have to meet the exacting standards of the organisation. If he failed, his reputation would be shot. John was an excellent cook working on instinct and this time he would have to play by the rulebook. The problem was compounded by the fact that while there were numerous books on the subject, there was no defining recipe. Should he use breadcrumbs for the crunchy topping? Should he use chicken or pork for the stock? Toulouse or not Toulouse sausage? He had walked into a minefield of researching, eating and breathing cassoulet, with every mention of the word rousing different emotions in the locals. And then there was a breakthrough. Having mentioned his dilemma to his friend Madame Bondouy, who ran a vegetable stall at the local market, she puffed out her bosom and told him there was nothing she did not know about cassoulet—and she would prove so by making it for him. She was in her element, clapping her hands excitedly as John ran around her kitchen like a commis chef, slicing, cutting, chopping and dicing. As to the ingredients, there was salami, black pudding, saucisson, chicken stock, pork belly, duck … ah, and handfuls of breadcrumbs. Then John made the mistake of mentioning the Confrérie. She thought it all complete nonsense. She made the best cassoulet in the region, so what did they know? There endeth the lesson for John, as he headed back to the drawing board.

Days later and in desperate need of direction, he rang another friend, Jean-Louis, and explained his recipe dilemma. No saucisson and definitely no breadcrumbs, he was told. The crunchy breast was a result of the fat bubbling and splitting the outside husk of the beans as they cooked. As for the stock, that was made from duck fat, pork bones, chicken bones, shin of veal and pig's trotters. Satisfied at last, all John now had to do was pass the acid test: serving to 20 people in a barn on the road between Castelnaudary and Villasavary, which belonged to one of the Confrérie members. The cassoulet went into a clay pot and was placed on an old-fashioned stove to keep warm. As the tasting began, silence fell in the barn. Then the comments started flowing. Negative at first. It was a bit salty and the beans were slightly overdone. But then came the positives. The pork was nice, and the piece de résistance … 'It's superb!' And finally, the big moment as meat supplier Antonio Spanghero stood and told the assembled diners that Mr. John Burton-Race had made an excellent cassoulet, and he decreed that he become a member of the great Cassoulet Confrérie. John's award was a medal and a special tile upon which he could place future cassoulets on.

CASSOULET
(Serves 8)

Ingredients

STOCK
1kg pork bones (from the loin, belly or chest)
2 pig's trotters
1kg shin of veal

1kg chicken pieces
3 litres water
1 onion, peeled and chopped
1 carrot, peeled and chopped
2 celery sticks, peeled and roughly chopped
1 leek, washed and chopped
1 garlic bulb, peeled and chopped
1 bay leaf
2 sprigs fresh thyme
2 sprigs flat-leaf parsley
1 tsp black peppercorns

BEANS

750g dried white kidney beans, soaked overnight
100g pork loin fat, cut into strips
1.5 litres water
2 sprigs fresh thyme
1 bay leaf
Half garlic bulb, halved

MEATS

4 small duck legs
1kg piece of pork (loin, belly for chest)
150g coarse sea salt
3 juniper berries, crushed
1 sprig fresh thyme, leaves picked from the stalks
1 bay leaf
2 garlic cloves, peeled and crushed
1 dessertspoon black peppercorns, crushed
8 Toulouse sausages

SAUTÉ

2 tbsp cooking fat, from the pork and duck
1 onion, peeled and chopped
3 large tomatoes, skinned, seeded and chopped

2 garlic cloves, peeled and finely chopped

1 sprig fresh thyme

2 bay leaves

175g white breadcrumbs

Method

1. For the stock, ask your butcher to chop the pork bones into small pieces. Put the trotters, veal, chicken and all the bones into a large, lidded saucepan. Cover them with cold water and bring to the boil. Add the vegetables, garlic, herbs and peppercorns, and bring back to the boil. Skim off any fat that rises to the surface and turn the stock down to a simmer. Cook, covered, for at least 4 hours, until the meat starts to fall off the shin.

2. Strain the stock into another saucepan and boil to reduce the liquid by half. You need 1.5 litres of finished stock for eight people.

3. Wash the beans and strain, then place in a saucepan, cover with more water and bring to the boil. Cook at a rapid boil for 5 minutes, then strain again.

4. Put the beans back into the pan, add the pork fat and cover with water. Add the thyme, bay leaf and garlic, and bring to the boil. Turn down to a simmer, cover and cook for about 1.5 hours, until tender and nearly all the water has evaporated. Most of the fat will have been absorbed into the beans. Remove what's left. Pick out the bay leaf, thyme and garlic, and discard. Set the beans aside.

5. Put the duck legs in a deep roasting tin. With a knife, remove the rind from the pork and add the meat to the tin. Mix the salt, juniper berries, thyme, bay leaf, garlic and peppercorns, and sprinkle over the duck and pork. Cover the tin with cling film and put in the fridge overnight.

6. In the morning, remove the bay leaf and thyme and, under cold running water, wash all the salt from the duck and pork. Dry the meat on a clean tea towel.

7. Meanwhile, pre-heat oven to 180°C/350°F/Gas 4, then roast the duck and pork for 1.5 hours. Remove the meat from the oven, cut

the duck legs in half and slice the pork into 8 pieces roughly 1cm thick, then set aside on a plate.

8. For the sauté, heat the fat in a frying pan, add the onion and fry until golden. Add the tomatoes, garlic, thyme and bay leaves, and cook for 5 minutes. Tip the mixture into a large casserole dish.
9. Pre-heat oven to 200°C/400°F/Gas 6.
10. In a frying pan, brown the sausages in some more of the fat and place them in the casserole.
11. Pour in the stock, then place the pork and duck in the casserole, and sprinkle in the beans. Cover with the breadcrumbs and cook in the oven for about an hour until crisp and golden. Serve.

With the farmhouse having been given a fresh coat of paint and the children settled at school, the family slowly settled into their new lives. It was not all wine and roses, however. While he gave off the appearance of a happily married man, John began to consider himself as nothing more than the lodger. He was in a fiery relationship. Kim was lonely and the kids initially hated leaving their schools and friends behind and made no secret of the fact that they resented him for dragging them across the Channel. As far as Kim was concerned, her husband had alienated her from what she particularly enjoyed- the theatre and shopping. It made for great television, however, with the rows and tantrums and John's boozy days away. The observant Pat Llewellyn commented that John was extremely good at dividing people. 'There's no doubt about that. His explosions can be quite shocking, but a bit of that is theatre. He laughs his head off when he looks at the tapes. That takes the sting out of it. He's always propelling forward in the most extraordinary way. He's in a hurry. The words "settling down" don't apply,' she told writer Rachael Cooke.

One day, John woke up in France with all these people around him and realised that he didn't actually like his wife anymore. Here he goes again, you might think, and you would be right: déjà vu. 'You fall in lust,' he admits, almost apologetically. 'When I met Kim, it was at a time of no girlfriends and no sex, and I was still married to Marie-Christine. It was simply job, job, job, because that has always been good to me. I have always been able to get back everything that I put into it. With everything going on in the house, however, and with a television crew in situ, there was enormous pressure not only on myself, but also on Kim. She loved playing up to the camera and she enjoyed the fame that came later on, and she was also very good at the privacy thing. I am not very good at that, but I coped with it and would simply take myself off. I was just like, "Off he goes, running away".'

John met some wonderful people in France and made sure he always had his hand-held recorder with him, dictating tales in preparation for the book. Sometimes he didn't return home for two or three days because he was cooking for new-found friends, and Kim had to cope with that. But then, you get people who play up to the camera and people that are natural in front of the lens, but it's never as good as just being oneself. It was a completely different way of life for the both of them. It wasn't about the money or the car he was driving, or the clothes they were wearing. It was about the peasant in the countryside who understood more about the value of life and friendships than most ever do. Some of the food they concocted was not that great, while other meals were amazing. They made cheese, chocolates and bread at three in the morning. They accepted John readily into their world and he was mightily proud of that, which is why he cried his eyes out when they left it all behind. It is not normally a good idea to reflect on what might have been, but it still plays on his mind that he could have bought the ramshackle farmhouse, with its 300 acres, barns, abandoned scrubland, six bedrooms and salt-water swimming pool, and been happy—but that is not John Burton-Race.

'Perhaps the most important thing I've learnt is that food is a process of constant learning,' he wrote. 'My passion for it is not only back, but stronger than ever.' It was a journey he would always remember and treasure, but at the back of his mind he had already begun to wonder what lay ahead for him back across the Channel.

30

BACK TO THE FUTURE

WHILE JOHN's heart was forever in France, French Leave producer Pat Llewellyn convinced him there was no way in the world he could make a living in the middle of nowhere. He also had to factor in that Kim, a city girl at heart, wanted out of the alien lifestyle and refused to listen to anything he said. Returning to the UK in 2004, there was no John Burton-Race at The Landmark. In fact, there was nowhere for him to operate from at all. He was at yet another crossroads in his career. He knew it. Kim knew it, and so did Pat. It was not long before reality set in and he had to find work. French Leave was a success, with viewing figures rising for each episode and book sales going through the roof, and the promise of a follow-up series to mark what he did next was in the offing. An initial proposal was to send John and the family to Spain. While he was up for it, no one else in the family was prepared to go with him. An idea was then floated that John could start a small business, and recordings would made about him searching for the premises, of the launch and the inevitable family squabbles, while adding up how much money he hadn't got or was making and what he could and couldn't afford.

John spent weeks driving around the furthest reaches of Devon trying to find somewhere to live. He loved the county's geography, seeing more sheep than people, and then there was the wonderful coastline and the seafood. At first, he was drawn to Salcombe, tempted by the fact that 65 per cent of people that lived there also had homes in London's westerly suburbs. He then discovered that the Meteorological Office in Exeter had upwards of 2,000 employees, and looking at the city's demographic, he noted that the town of Topsham, two miles from the centre, was a particularly affluent area. With its lovely Dutch-gabled and Georgian houses, John was nine-tenths down the road of buying a large Italian restaurant in the town when he was approached by the owner of the Carved Angel in Dartmouth, who wanted out. John's immediate thought was that if he could go into a place that had a fabulous reputation in the area and bring a modern-day food offering, that would be both quicker and easier for him to make his mark.

Dartmouth is a popular year-round haven for food lovers who arrive in search of the county's generous larder, from seafood to ice cream and fudge. John realised it was the perfect launch pad to set up shop, reinvigorated after his two-year self-imposed culinary exile in the French countryside. The Carved Angel, previously the home of the legendary cook Joyce Molyneux, was housed in a half-timbered building on the quay. The plan was to take on the restaurant and re-shape it in his image, delivering to diners some of the ideas he'd picked up across the Channel. If he hadn't seen quite enough of camera crews over the previous year, the new fly-on-the-wall television series was confirmed and to be called Return Of The Chef. Once again it would feature family fortunes, misfortunes and frequent fallouts while showcasing John's lively, mercurial nature. Kim labelled him Satan in the trailers.

When it comes to notable celebrity chefs, Dartmouth can certainly lay claim to a few. It was here that Keith Floyd found notoriety. He was a unique, hugely likeable, flamboyant but ultimately flawed man who amassed a huge following on television. In a crisp white shirt and dickie bow, he prowled the kitchen with a ladle in one hand, slopping food into large bowls, while consuming vast quantities of red wine, constantly telling his cameraman Clive to come closer so he could catch the action of his pot-stirring genius. His celebrated TV career began with Floyd On Food. In the 1990s, Floyd poured £1 million into the Maltsters Arms, an 18th century riverside pub in the hamlet of Tuckenhay, nestling in the splendid Dart Valley. He married a Dartmouth girl but after a series of splits and reconciliations, they divorced in 1994. Eventually, and almost inevitably, Floyd went bankrupt. He died five years later, lambasting the UK brigade of celebrity chefs of whom he had in no small part paved the way for.

Joyce Molyneux was at the head of the tide of celebrity chef status in Dartmouth, having first surfaced at the Hole In The Wall in Bath, owned by Lancastrian restaurateur George Perry Smith. In 1973, Perry Smith travelled to Dartmouth to check out a mock-Tudor building on the South Embankment. A year later it opened as the Carved Angel and quickly established a reputation as the finest restaurant in the country. Humble Molyneux was no doubt taken aback by her ascendancy, with chefs drawn like a magnet to savour the food created by a woman who claimed she never wrote a single recipe but was a magpie, taking the best bits of other people's ideas.

The restaurant was named so when Molyneux was presented with a carved wooden angel by a local carpenter during refurbishment of the property. Completely taken with the beautiful carving, she placed it in the dining room for her guests to admire. Molyneux hung up her apron for the final time in 1999 to enjoy retirement, which wasn't to last for she had already begun a new career as a judge on the original MasterChef television series. One of the first women in the UK to receive a Michelin star, Molyneux's first cookbook sold 50,000 copies. Recently interviewed by Jay Rayner for The Guardian as part of the newspaper's Seven Ages Of A Chef series, she offered the following advice to young cooks: 'Just enjoy yourself, the food, the cooking and the company.'

John tells me, 'I like to think that buying the restaurant was something that was meant to be.' The first thing on his mind was the actual name. While he could have kept it as the Carved Angel, he did not want to because the name would always be associated with Molyneux, whom he knew and very much respected. With a name change in place, it was clear from the outset that his reputation preceded him, thanks in large part to his exposure on television in French Leave, and the New Angel soon gained a reputation for its superb cuisine. From the outset the plan was to open the restaurant as a family business, where daughter Eve would work in the office and the other girls would act as waitresses on Saturday evenings. As business partner with Kim, John bought the freehold and placed it in a trust, with equal voting rights. The first week of trading saw 540 covers pass through the kitchen, and in only its first month the restaurant received a Michelin star.

John's time in France made him realise that food did not have to be fancy to be good. 'I rediscovered the pleasures of cooking and eating simple, no-fuss dishes made from seasonal local ingredients—the kind of food that had an honesty I felt I had somehow lost sight of in my years as a Michelin-star chef,' he wrote in Coming Home, a book based on Return Of The Chef.

During the season from May to the end of September, bass was everywhere in Dartmouth and proved to be particularly popular with diners. The fish was also a favourite of his friend, the late Pat Llewelyn.

WHOLE GRILLED SEA BASS IN SALT PASTRY
(Serves 6)

Ingredients

3 x 750-800g sea bass
50g dill or fennel top
1 egg, beaten together with 30ml milk, for egg wash
30g unsalted butter, melted
(Salt Crust Pastry)
1kg plain flour
600g table salt
20g dried fennel seeds
300ml egg whites (about 10 eggs)
300ml water

Method

1. First make the salt crust pastry. Sieve the flour into the bowl of a food mixer and attach the dough hook. Add the salt and fennel seeds and mix together with the motor set at its lowest speed. Add the egg whites and continue mixing for 2-3 minutes. Gradually

add the water and mix until you have a smooth pastry that comes away cleanly from the sides of the bowl. Stop the machine, turn out the pastry and wrap it up tightly in cling film. Put to one side to rest for at least 30 minutes.

2. Preheat the oven to 220°C/425°F/Gas 7.

3. Clean, gut and scale the bass. With a pair of fish scissors, cut off the fins and trim the tail fins. Dry the remaining fish on some kitchen paper.

4. Lightly dust a work surface with a little flour. Cut the salt crust into six equal pieces and, in turn, cut these in half. Roll out each piece into a rectangle 32 x 20cm, with a thickness of about 5mm. Lay the bass lengthways in the middle of three of the rectangles. Place some dill or fennel tops into the stomach of the fish. Dip a small pastry brush into cold water and brush around the edges of the pastry. Place a second piece of pastry over the fish and, using the sides of your hands, gently mould and shape the pastry so that the contours of the fish are visible. Press the edges down firmly to seal the pastry tightly; there must not be any holes. The fish cooks in its own steam and if there are any holes in the pastry you will not achieve the correct result. Cut away the overlapping excess pastry around the fish. When doing this, re-model the fins and cut out the tail. Leave a border of about 1cm of pastry between the fins to allow for shrinkage during cooking. With the back of a knife, score the fins to give a more authentic appearance. Take some of the excess pastry, roll it out and cut another fin. With the pastry brush, brush a little more water just behind the gill and press this on to the pastry. Mould an eye, and again, with a little water, stick it in place. Gently drag the point of your knife along the middle of the fish, stopping just at the back of the head. To mould some scales, start at the tail of the fish and, with the point of your knife, pit the pastry all the way up to the head. Repeat this process several times for maximum effect but be very careful not to puncture the pastry. Brush the pastry with egg wash and place on a baking tray.

5. Cook in the preheated oven for 17 minutes, then remove the fish from the oven and brush the salt crust with the melted butter. Transfer the fish to a board and present them to the table.

6. To remove the fish from the pastry, cut, using a sharp knife, around the outer edge of the crust (the skin will automatically come away as well). With a sharp knife and fork, remove the top fillet to a serving plate. Remove and discard the exposed backbone, gently lift out the remaining fillet and place on another plate. Serve immediately.

'It is obvious, even after only eight months, that the New Angel is, and will continue to be, a huge success. The menu is so good—so deliciously unfussy—that it is almost impossible to choose (for the record, I had lobster lasagne with mussel and saffron sauce). It was already in the Good Food Guide, but when the TV series began, the NEW Angel became a destination restaurant,' noted journalist Rachael Cooke.

A Sunday lunchtime favourite was roasted loin of pork served with a stuffed or baked apple with prunes, complemented by Devon dry cider for the sauce. To prepare this dish, John recommends asking your butcher to remove the rib and chine bones and chop them up small, as they will be needed for the sauce. Also ask your butcher to tie the loin for roasting. This recipe is delicious with young buttered spinach, glazed carrots and roast or mashed potatoes.

ROAST LOIN OF PORK WITH PRUNES AND APPLE
(Serves 6)

Ingredients
1.5-2kg loin of pork
Salt and freshly milled black pepper
2 tbsp groundnut oil

(FOR THE SAUCE)
2tbsp groundnut oil
500g pork bones, chopped small

1 onion, chopped
1 carrot, peeled and chopped
1 stick celery, chopped
2 garlic cloves, peeled and crushed
½ bay leaf
. 2 sprigs thyme
2 Granny Smith apples
200ml dry cider
400ml chicken stock

(APPLES)
5 Granny Smith apples
35g unsalted butter
35g soft brown sugar
12 prunes
1 pinch cinnamon
2 tbsp Calvados or brandy
Lemon sauce

Method

1. Preheat the oven to 200°C/400°F/Gas 6.
2. Rub salt into the rind of the pork to get a good, crisp crackling, then season with pepper. Put a large roasting pan on the stove to heat. Add the groundnut oil and as soon as it starts to smoke, carefully place the pork into the oil. Seal and lightly colour the pork, then place in the oven for about 1 hour 20 minutes.
3. Next make the sauce. Put a large saucepan on the stove to heat. Add the oil and as soon as it starts to smoke, add the bones and fry them until golden brown in colour. Add the onion, carrot, celery, garlic, bay leaf and thyme, and fry until coloured brown. Chop the apples, including the cores, and add them to the pan. Pour in the cider, and boil until its volume has been reduced by half, or until the apples become soft. Pour in the chicken stock and bring it back to the boil. With a ladle, skim off the surfacing sediment and discard. Reduce the heat to a moderate simmer.

4. Cut three of the five Granny Smith apples in half (horizontally) and core them. Place in a buttered baking dish, cut side up, sprinkle with half the brown sugar and bake in the oven for about 10 minutes to soften.

5. Peel and core the remaining apples and coarsely cut them into a bowl. Split the prunes and remove the stones. Cut them into small strips and add them to the grated apple, together with the cinnamon, the remaining brown sugar and butter, the Calvados and a little lemon juice. Mix all the ingredients together well. Remove the par-baked apples from the oven and fill them with the prune mixture. Reduce the oven temperature to 180°C/350°F/Gas 4 and bake for a further 25 minutes. Time this with the cooking of the pork.

6. Meanwhile, strain the sauce through a fine sieve into another saucepan, then bring back up to the boil. With a ladle, skim off any surfacing sediment and discard. Continue to boil the sauce until its volume has been reduced by half. The sauce will start to thicken as it reduces, and the flavour of the apples and cider will start to come through.

7. Remove the loin of pork from the oven and place it on a serving plate or board to rest. Carefully pour off the fat from the roasting pan and place the pan on the stove. Pour in the sauce and bring it back to the boil to collect all the meat juices. Strain the sauce through another fine sieve lined with a piece of muslin cloth to trap all the sediment. Arrange the baked apples around the pork. Bring the dish to the table with the sauce served separately in a sauce boat.

31

ANGEL IN FREEFALL

THE IRONY was not lost on John that by 2005, within four months of opening, the New Angel had not only gained its first Michelin star but was voted AA Restaurant of the Year. Success bred success. The whole cycle was self-perpetuating. And yet, yet ... John wasn't sure whether he was ready for that first Michelin star in such a short space of time. He had been struggling to pay the bills and he almost felt guilty that perhaps there were chefs more worthy of the prestigious accolade. 'It was like, everyone wants to know you when you are winning the fight, but the first time you lose, no one wants to know you, but then maybe I take myself a bit too seriously and yes, maybe I am too cynical, as I would rather suspect bullshit before realising there is anything genuine behind something,' he tells me.

Interestingly, at the end of the first year of trading, 62 per cent of telephone bookings had been associated with London numbers. Diners would make a pilgrimage to their second homes in the country. Those with homes in Cornwall would enjoy a gourmet cruise, taking in restaurants including the New Angel and Rick Stein's The Seafood Restaurant in Padstow. Dartmouth simply imploded from John's presence, and suddenly everyone else was getting rich on his back. But then most things have a certain shelf life and he was well aware of that. Consistency is the key, which is one reason why he holds in such great respect the Roux brothers at The Waterside, Michel Roux Junior's Le Gavroche, and Raymond Blanc at Le Manoir. To be in the same place and still make somewhere successful as a business without pomp or ceremony or television is no mean feat. While The Waterside Inn, one of the grand old ladies, continued to prosper, there was the New Angel, which probably had a six or seven-year shelf life. It was not as if John had lost interest or discontinued his progression in cooking ability; it was more that people were looking for the next model and the next colour, and the New Angel remained the same. Diners will only go to a restaurant if they can afford it.

The industry and the individual restaurant are affected by the economic climate and people's pockets, so it is a tremendously hard business and even though one might deliver consistency, sometimes that is simply not enough. 'Trading in Dartmouth is not like Sercombe,' says John. 'In Dartmouth we may be trading for seven, possibly eight months of the year, but then we would have three months where we were doing nothing. It is cold and wet, and people with disposable income do not come down in the winter so you have to rely on the local clientele. Since my time at the New Angel I imagine things have got better, because more people have moved out of London and made Devon their permanent home. Now poor old Dad, if he can't work at home on his computer, must travel back to London during the week and stay in a bedsit. Today I believe there is a missed opportunity in the restaurants and pubs around here of ladies for lunch. I don't mean steak and kidney pie, but a glass of champagne and a calorie-conscious salad. No one is doing it. We have these middle and upper-middle class ladies with children at the local private or public school with not a lot to do. It's very clique, and we are a little in the Dark Ages because there is all that money which remains untapped. When I had the New Angel, that circle of wealth was only half full whereas now it is three-quarters full. In the West Country today there are possibly half-a-dozen good hotels and restaurants of the higher echelon that weren't around when I opened, but then sometimes it is hard to be first.'

At the New Angel, January was usually a total write-off and yet John was employing staff on a full-time basis, where most businesses were running mostly part-timers. To maintain standards, he was paying London wages, so even with hardly any custom he was continuing to roll out the payroll from a dwindling bank account, and yet that was precisely the time when renovations needed to be done. February was the same. In fact, nothing much would happen until Easter. John realised that by taking on the New Angel, while he may have escaped the rat race that was London, all he had really done was swapped a large hamster wheel for a smaller one and was simply paddling faster. And yet while the business side of things was looking far from rosy, he was very conscious that on the creative side, the suppliers remained second-to-none. In London he would pay twice as much for sea bass. In Dartmouth it was far more laid back. He would ask a fisherman how many lobsters he was going to get and would be told that he had no idea until the pots were hove to.

A certain Nigel Marriage also hove to at the New Angel, where John brought him in as head chef. 'He was a great cook but a madman, and while I admired how he went about life, he was not popular. I know I had my enemies, but he was off the scale,' says John of his friend. As for the rest of the team, John took advantage of the falling economy in Italy. With that country's declining economy in freefall, London in particular was awash with Italians seeking employment. As a result, five Italians made up his team of nine. At half his age, they ended up showing John things in the kitchen he had never seen in his life. He incorporated what they knew and in return showed them what he knew, and as a result the food went in a completely different direction. James Willis was a case in point. His previous position had been at The Lanesborough, a Regency-style luxury hotel a mere two-minute walk from London's Hyde Park Corner and 12 minutes from all the upscale shopping in Knightsbridge. It must have been a serious culture shock to find himself by the River Dart in sleepy Devon. Having worked with James previously, John was well aware of his talent but because the two got on so well together, it caused friction between John and the other members of staff. Aware of the fact, he tried not to let it show. There was also friction between Willis and Stephen Humphreys, who had joined the kitchen team. With a Scottish mother and his father being a former American Seal, Willis had developed a broad American accent and knew all the New York insults. John loved it when he was in a rant during service. He would come out with a host of expletives you would not normally hear in England.

'We tend to forget that if we have a shit night in the kitchen, that doesn't necessarily translate into a shit night in the restaurant,' John tells me. 'The great thing is that when you are performing at that level every night, we aspire to get everything out as perfect as possible. That is not only the perfectionist in us all, but also the professionalism. I would tell my staff that even though we may have had a tough night, the customers would be the ones to put things in perspective.' Even so, John would beat himself up about it. It was in his nature. He learned from the late French chef Bernard Loiseau that diners having a good night was key. Loiseau shot himself in 2003, having worked a full day in the kitchen, when the French newspaper Le Figaro hinted that his restaurant La Cote d'Or might lose one its three Michelin stars. Loiseau had already suffered at the hands of the Gault Millau guide, which had downgraded his restaurant from 19/20 to 17/20. Loiseau had previously resisted the new, populist form of Asian-inspired fusion cuisine sweeping through France and was conscious that his cuisine and philosophy was being superseded by the newer trend appealing to international foodies. He spent the best part of 17 years aiming to achieve his ambition of becoming a three-star chef. Ever conscious of his restaurant's decreasing patronage and rising debts, he told chef Jacques Lameloise, 'If a lose a star, I will kill myself.' That tragedy hit John hard, although he remains reconciled to the fact that while you may believe you have done your best, you cannot please everybody. 'Chefs acted differently compared to today,' he says. 'There is nothing more public than who has won or lost a Michelin star, and it is a poor culture to be in. You cannot hold on to something forever, and there will always be a generation who think they are better than you and are therefore more worthy. They tend to forget all the shit we will have gone through to get the recognition. As you get older you tend not to worry about it so much. All I want to make sure of is that I have happy customers.'

There is not only a human story behind every gain and loss, but also a reality which plays out through the business and the markets. With so many restaurants that are not even starred but doing well, John is aware you cannot run a restaurant simply to try and gain a Michelin star. Today, many restaurants do not want the pressure that comes with a star of keeping it or losing it. It is a blessing and a curse. 'You have to accept that there will always be restaurants that are more popular for whatever reason,' he says. 'It may not be just about the food. For the top 50 restaurants in the world, it is as much about a PR stunt as it is about anything else. It can become both a psychological problem and a burden if you let it get to you. That is why you have to have the self-confidence in yourself of who you are and what you do.'

I asked John's daughter Naomi if she had any recollection of her father's success, both as a restaurateur and celebrity chef. Naomi left for France with her mother and brother when she was 14. I remember that when I was younger and still living in England, on rare occasions people used to talk about Dad. Other than that, growing up I don't believe I was truly aware that he was a celebrity. Having left for France, I missed the period when he received important exposure with programmes like French Leave and MasterChef and was oblivious to what was happening on television in Britain. To be honest, it was only when I was 18 or 19 that I would hear what was going on in the UK and what he was up to via the few contacts I had left in England. That was the time he was at The Landmark in London, and the first time I tried to contact him.'

One evening while at a friend's house preparing for a night out, Naomi was surfing the internet searching for her father's contact details. Unable to find anything, she thought the only way to contact him would be to book a table at the restaurant, which she did. In the comments section of the online book-ing form she wrote a short message in which she introduced herself. 'Nothing happened after that reservation,' she tells me. 'The second time I tried to contact Dad happened during a trip to Devon. I read a few articles about him and wanted to see if I could see him in Dartmouth. I explained the plan to Mum and we made a day trip out of it. We visited Dartmouth, the port and the castle, and found his restaurant on the seafront. Telling myself that I had nothing to lose, I went in and Mum accompanied me. As soon as we got in the main room on the ground floor there was a commotion in the kitchen. My mother explained later that Nigel (Marriage), who had worked at L'Ortolan had recognised us, panicked and left. We were greeted by a young lady who gave me a piece of paper and pen for me to write a message to Dad, who was absent at that time. So that's what I did. I presented myself and gave my contact details for him to call back.'

John did just that, perhaps six months later, one evening out of the blue. 'It was awkward because we didn't know what to say,' recalls Naomi. 'Occasional phone calls and messages took place after that. We met when he came to France on holiday a few years later after his divorce (from Kim), when Pip (John's son with third wife Suzi) was already seven or eight. I took a train to Avignon and he came to meet me at the station.' Today, John and Naomi share a good relationship and she tells me, 'We are alike in many ways. From a positive perspective I would say he is very talented and passionate about what he does. He is extremely kind and generous. He is also quite the introvert, despite what he shows on television. He is also the biggest drama queen I have ever met!'

With the New Angel basking in its initial success and the television series proving as popular as French Leave had done, Ebury Press gained the rights to publish the book based on the prime-time television series Coming Home. Packed with more than 150 easy-to-make-recipes, the food did not call for complicated ingredients or hours spent in the kitchen. Spending time in the Aude region of southwestern France, John understood that food did not have to be fancy to be good. He rediscovered the honesty of food and did not want to leave those feelings behind in France. 'Although this book is primarily a celebration of the produce of Devon, I also like to think of it as a tribute to the best that Britain, as a whole, has to offer,' he wrote in the foreword. During fleeting moments of leisure, John enjoyed fishing for mackerel at Slapton beach, at the point the furthest away from Torcross. He chose to include one of his favourite recipes for the book.

PAN-FRIED MACKEREL WITH GOOSBERRIES
(Serves 4)

Ingredients
400g gooseberries
60g unsalted butter
50g caster sugar
25g root ginger, peeled, and finely chopped or grated
Zest of 1 orange
4 medium-sized mackerel
Salt
Freshly milled black pepper
2 tbsp olive oil

Method
1. Wash the gooseberries and drain them through a colander. Melt half the butter in a small, lidded pan and add the sugar. Stir in the fruit, then add the ginger and orange zest. Cover with the lid and cook over a gentle heat for about 5 minutes. Remove the lid and turn up the heat to evaporate the liquid, stirring occasionally. This will take a further 10 minutes. Keep warm.

2. Cut open the stomachs of the mackerel from the vent to the gills. Remove the insides of the fish and discard. Cut out the gills and, with a pair of fish scissors, cut off the fins and discard. Wash the fish under cold running water and dry with kitchen paper. Turn the fish on its side and fillet it, cutting either side of the backbone. Discard the bone and, using a pair of tweezers, pin-bone the fillets. Turn the mackerel fillets over and make a few shallow cuts across the skin, to aid even cooking. Season the fillets with salt and pepper.

3. Place a large frying pan on the stove to heat. Pour in the olive oil and as soon as it starts to smoke, lay the mackerel, flesh side down, into the oil. Fry for 3-4 minutes until coloured golden brown,

then turn them over and cook for a further 2 minutes. Add the remaining butter. They are ready as soon as the butter has melted and started to foam.

4. Take the pan off the heat and using a fish slice, remove the fillets and lay them on four serving plates. Serve immediately, with a spoonful of the gooseberry sauce on each plate.

Despite the success of the television series and the accompanying book, problems once again came knocking, much of it due to the restaurant's pricing issues. While the finances were woefully bad, John's head remained in his menus and he was fixated on delivering food par excellence. Prized fish such as crab and lobster were virtually being given away. Additionally, John was unhappy with his front-of-house team, so they had to go, replaced by a virtual French team. Rammed for lunch and dinner every day, and a £1.4 million turnover on food in its first year, still nothing went according to plan. The New Angel was a shop window for his extraordinary creativity, feted by the best ingredients the county of Devon could offer up, but it was a financial disaster. Things were complicated by the fact that John's relationship with Kim was at breaking point. As he was to tell Rachael Cooke, 'I've had a wife who's in business and that has its problems, and I've had a wife who isn't in the business, and that has its problems. I'm not saying chefs are better off alone. They need someone to care for them, too. But if you're attracted to the madness of a chef, the excitement of him, why spend all your life trying to shape him into being someone else? Get another bloke.'

The eventual breakdown resulted in an acrimonious and hugely expensive divorce in which John lost everything, including the pension he worked so hard for. The final nail in the coffin came after Kim discovered that John had been in another relationship for two years, a relationship which also involved a child. 'There is nothing quite like a woman scorned,' he says. 'My ex-wife had some really shabby friends in London whom I despised. I very quickly grew to dislike her, but then I began to dislike myself even more for being such a wanker. Kim was not my type.' It must have hurt but he never let it show. Never reveal your hand to the enemy. So instead he rolled with the punches, and there were plenty of them. Battered and bruised, he took sustenance from the fact that two good things had resulted from the marriage: his children Amelia and Charles. 'Charles is bright academically. He had a good job with the American multinational finance and insurance corporation AIG, which he gave up so he could return to university to study history,' he tells me. 'He rang me up one day and told me he had resigned because he was bored. I told him he was silly, as he would struggle to get a job again. He replied that it was not about the money, and I thought that's the sort of thing I would say, so I told him to go ahead. Amelia is the polar opposite and not unlike her mother. If you buy her a £1,500 handbag, she'd still want another one! She has the killer instinct. I have to say that Kim has done a great job with the both of them, as they are fairly grounded, even though I believe she has tried desperately to poison them against me.'

Having arranged to meet Amelia and Charles for this biography, they both then declined, allegedly following their mother's insistence that they must not be involved; a shame as it would have been nice to see their side of the story.

32

SECRET LIAISONS

IN FEBRUARY 2004, Suzi Ward was working from her home office at Asherne Cottage, a delightful property on the A379 in the village of Strete, with stunning views over the English Channel. Suzi had a successful small business making greetings cards. Answering her telephone, at the other end was John Burton-Race's agents, Burnley Staine Spear, with whom she had worked previously for ten years. Asked if she knew who John was, she replied she remembered him from French Leave. Suzi was told that John had purchased the Carved Angel and a production company was planning a new series, and the family needed somewhere to live. Suzi was acquainted with several people who owned large houses in the area, and she was asked to enquire if anyone might rent their property for six months. The production company, they said, would use the home as one of the prime filming locations.

Suzi contacted close friend Caroline Murray, who owned a medieval farmhouse with plenty of bedrooms at Netherton. Caroline said she would think about the proposition. Later the same day Suzi received a further call from the agents, stating John would be travelling from his home in Reading to Devon the next day, and asked if she could arrange a viewing of the property. With John's mobile number to hand, she made contact. Suzi arranged for them to meet at the Dart Marina Hotel and Spa. 'I remember it well. My four-wheel-drive is always full of horse rugs and dogs. I was thinking this chap is from London and he is going to be smart, and therefore would not want to sit in my vehicle with all its resident smells,' Suzi tells me. 'My friend Simon offered me the loan of his short-wheel-base Land Rover, one step up from my Toyota Land Cruiser. I turned up in this green vehicle, and John arrived in his Audi S4. I introduced myself and asked if he wanted to travel with me, but he declined politely, commenting, "I think we will take my car".'

Suzi chose the scenic coast route, offering John a guided tour of the splendid countryside. Arriving at Caroline's lime-washed, mustard-coloured house, John was impressed immediately, and Caroline made them welcome with a cup of coffee. Suzi confesses that Caroline doesn't make the best coffee in the world, which is possibly more akin to drinking bilge, which was reflected in John's face when Suzi saw him pulling a face as he gently sipped. He was there to look at the house, however, not drink coffee, and what he saw was enough for him to exchange contact details with Caroline. On the return journey, John asked Suzi whether she might like to have lunch. They called in at the Floating Bridge, situated near where the Higher Ferry operates between Dartmouth and Kingswear. It just so happened to be pouring with rain, and few people had ventured out for lunch. It was here that the pair began a long tradition of eating pie and chips. On this, their first occasion dining together, they enjoyed steak and kidney pie and chips. Suzi introduced John to real ale, steering him away from his usual preference for lager. After lunch, John said he had to look at the independent Tower House School in Paignton for the children. As he drove his car on to the ferry, Suzi headed off in the opposite direction, thinking that that would be the end of the matter.

It wasn't. A couple of days later, John rang Suzi to say he was due to visit the county again and asked if she might like to have supper. Suzi recalls him being particularly forthright, asking where she lived. He said she could choose any restaurant and he'd pick her up at 7pm. Normally, whenever Suzi heard anyone walking up the garden path to the cottage, the gate would swing back with a 'ching' noise and her three dogs would bark. On the evening in question, Suzi was upstairs getting ready when she heard the gate go. It was about 6.30pm and she thought it was her neighbour Pam, but then she heard John shouting from the bottom of the stairs. 'I could see him looking around and no doubt thinking to himself, "What the bloody hell is this?".'

The couple went to the Tower Inn in Slapton and enjoyed guinea fowl. John ordered a nice bottle of wine. 'Whatever the bottle of wine was, it should have been a 2002 year, but it was the wrong year on the wine list. The right year should have sold for £30, and the wrong year, £15. John kicked off straight away, saying it was wrong,' recalls Suzi. After dinner they drove back to village and called in at the pub where they were later joined by one of Suzi's friends. Again, she thought that would be the end of it, imagining that when John moved to Dartmouth, she would probably eat in his restaurant, including for her 39th birthday party.

The meetings and cosy dinners became more than the mere passing of pleasantries and eyes across the table. 'I realised this was quite serious now,' John tells me. 'Both Suzi and I needed to decide that we needed to stay together no matter what.' And a short while later, Suzi discovered she was pregnant. It was a total shock to them both, and Suzi in particular thought it ridiculous. She had a young horse she had just broken in and was going to start hunting her. She thought, 'I don't really need this. I like children but I had never seen the necessity for having them.' Aged 38, she thought the situation completely mad. She didn't even know the man. To conceal the situation, Suzi used the code name Oliver Hanbury for John. As it happened, she had a long-time friend called Hanbury in London, and as she was making regular trips there, it made perfect sense. Suzi told people the father of her unborn child was Oliver Hanbury, and he remained so for some considerable time. 'Neither of us realised there was birth control in Devon in 2004!' says John. 'We decided to have our son Pip because we loved each other. And as for Suzi feeling like "the other woman", Suzi's not like other women. She would never feel like "the other woman". Suzi is just Suzi.'

In 2005, Suzi and John's relationship was very much established, but discreet. 'In our minds we planned to be together,' says John. 'However, at times it felt like a pipe dream. Being secretive was part of protecting each other.' John was involved in a television programme located in Beaunem, a walled town at the centre of the Burgundy winemaking region in France. 'I just so happened to be there with a girlfriend, and John and I just happened to meet at a café, surprise, surprise!' Suzi says. An extraordinary coincidence, but they were also booked into the same hotel, the five-star Hotel Le Cep & Spa. Suzi remembers it being 'dark and oaky, rather tired looking, but in a nice way'. With John out filming during the day, he suggested they meet for supper. On the first of three nights together, they enjoyed a meal at a one-star Michelin restaurant in a vineyard outside Beaunem. 'It was very modern French,' says Suzi. 'I had a squab pigeon dish. My meal was served in a bowl. I like food on a white plate so I can see what I am eating, I don't want to eat food off slates or in bowls. Restaurants do it all the time, trying to be clever and I don't know why. They had also used all types of Japanese spice, and yet we were in France, not Tokyo, and it didn't work. The following evening, we "bumped" into each other again and went to the L'Hostellerie de Levernois. We normally go there once a year on our route down to Provence. John had escargot en croute, made to a classic French recipe using jumbo helix snails, white wine, butter, parsley and copious amounts of garlic, all wrapped in premium quality puff pastry dough. I had a big piece of Limousin beef for the main.'

There is little wonder that later they became so enamoured with the region. 'Everything we love is there,' says John. 'Everyone will tell you that the best wines are from Bordeaux, but they are not our thing. We don't like heavy wine. You can get out of the car and immediately smell the wine. In the afternoons everywhere is closed, and it is wonderful to simply walk around. It is amazing. France is the most beautiful country in the world. It encompasses everything we love and wish to embrace, from the architecture to the space, the scenery, privacy, food and wine.'

33

UNFOLDING SOAP OPERA

THEIR SON Pip was born on December 17, 2004. John wasn't present at the birth, although he says that for once, Suzi was very quiet, and no expletives were expressed! She tells me that's because she was very scared. 'I telephoned the maternity unit throughout the day under the guise of James Beaver to ask how things were going,' recalls John, and Suzi remembers the midwife asking her, 'It's James Beaver again, what do you want to say?'

Meanwhile, John and his family were living a mere six miles from Suzi's cottage. 'It was like a soap opera,' she tells me. There was John, torn between two camps, his lover and child on the one side, his wife and children on the other. He found himself living a lie in a failing marriage; wanting to do the right thing, but how? He was acutely conscious that his first marriage to Marie-Christine had ended disastrously, through no fault of her own, and he had left the household and their two children behind. Now history was about to repeat itself.

John managed to see his son two or three times a week for the first couple of years of Pip's life. 'He always called me Daddy and sometimes when we were in a public place, I wish he hadn't! There was no question Mummy was Mummy and Daddy was Daddy,' says John. 'Suzi and I saw a lot of each other and often had trips away. We had a long time to think about our future and stayed together throughout this time of immense pressure. I can remember sitting on the observation deck of a P&O ferry from Dover to Calais with Suzi in the days when you could smoke on board, and looking across to the beaches of Calais full of holidaymakers having fun and both of us feeling free in the bright sunshine. Our excitement of going to France never changes.

'I had been portrayed as this great family man in French Leave—the chef with all those children—and it was very difficult when you have that image. Only two, of course, were mine, Charles and Amelia, the four other girls were from Kim's previous marriage.'

If the media, who had been actively hostile towards John in the past, got wind of the situation, they would no doubt go for the jugular again. He was adept at holding his own counsel, and Suzi, who'd done her utmost to keep the situation under wraps from friends and family, was a strong woman and was not one to suffer fools gladly. 'Suzi and I chose to keep our secret because we were very conscious that there would be adverse press and under the circumstances it would be rather difficult to explain. I have met several men who have been unfaithful and have continued with their lie all their lives. Some wait until the children have grown up, some break the relationship because married life is stronger than the affair and some end the affair as it may be financially damaging to all parties—and I know examples of all three! Eventually for me it got to the point when I had the courage to make the leap. We all strive for happiness and with that sometimes comes pain.' As the affair continued from one year to the next, John naively began to feel it would probably never come out. Suzi, however, did not, and warned him of the impending fallout. 'Nothing could ever prepare me for when it did,' says John.

The crunch came at 9am on Saturday, March 10, 2007, when John's wife read a text message from Suzi to John which simply read, 'Good morning X'. 'I had never done that before,' says Suzi. 'In a way I did it on purpose, thinking Kim might see it, because John and I had had about enough by this stage. I would never phone John, it was always the other way around. By this time, I am sure people were thinking Pip was John's child because you only have to look at him. A couple of very close friends of mine knew the truth, including Caroline, but they were extremely discreet. John phoned and said Kim had seen the text, and World War Three had broken out. He had always joked about that happening, but I think the fact that it was really bad took him by surprise.'

When Kim confronted John with the text, he refused to talk about it. With Suzi's landline number to hand, Kim, understandably hurt, rang and shared her anger. After a number of heated conversations, Suzi phoned British Telecom that same afternoon, requesting them to change her number. Informed that they couldn't do anything until the following Monday, Suzi turned the ringer off. The phone's light continued to flash continually as Kim tried to call. According to Suzi, it went on for the next 48 hours. That evening, John and Suzi decamped to a hotel in Exeter. Kim later told the Evening Standard, describing how she punched and scratched John in a blind fit of rage when he finally admitted to the affair. 'I tore the T-shirt off his back and screamed at him. Then he admitted he was going to live with her. I told him to get out. John showed no contrition. After he left, I made a bonfire of his clothes in the garden. Since he has gone, our home life is calmer, but the children and I feel totally betrayed.'

Far from the exposure of the affair bringing relief after living a lie for three years, it was another extremely difficult period in John's life. 'I'd decided to stay with Kim for those three years mainly because of Charles and Amelia, as they were both quite young at the time and I felt a great sense of guilt,' John tells me. 'I already knew that Kim and I were incompatible, but I kept going back because I'm sorry to say I was weak. The Press tried to destroy me. My reputation was ripped apart. For my part, it really affected me mentally and physically. I lost some of my self-esteem and for a period I was in quite a dark place. Suzi, on the other hand, was brilliant, strong and very prag-matic, all of which I admired. My guilt was already enormous, but I admit to what the Press did and how they depicted me—even when I knew most of it was untrue—still got to me. People who I had regarded as firm friends let me down. I was an easy target to have a pop at. We all know that life is sometimes cruel. For the main I've come through it. Suzi greatly helped, as did the thought of my children and, of course, my cooking. Not for the first time did my love of cooking get me through. Maybe it's escapism, but it's never let me down.' In many people's eyes he'd behaved badly and was now paying the penalty for his infidelity. He was certainly not the type to expect forgiveness or deliberately set about ingratiating himself with the public, but an opportunity arose.

That summer he reluctantly agreed to appear on I'm A Celebrity, Get Me Out Of Here, having declined the previous year due to work commitments. He had only watched the programme once, when Peter Andre and Jordan were canoodling on camera. Prior to flying to Australia with Suzi and Pip, a team from the show's production office took photographs of him at the New Angel and visited Suzi at their cottage. Taking in her lifestyle and where she lived, the crew said she would probably not enjoy herself on the other side of the world — not what she wanted to hear, but this was a chance to briefly escape the UK. No doubt the couple were conscious of the irony of appearing on one of the most popular shows on television, but to John, heading to the Australian jungle seemed like a good place, away from all the festering anger on home turf.

Come November and the start of filming, John found himself in a totally alien environment with celebrities he didn't know, and some he grew to dislike. And in their wake were the British paparazzi. Having devoured the gossip on his marriage break-up and secret child, they were hungry for more. With John deep in the jungle, reporters and photographers swarmed around Suzi who, to her credit, did not buckle under the incessant pressure to tell her story. 'I didn't want anyone to know what I was doing. I simply didn't need it,' she tells me. 'I didn't want to find myself in newspapers and I didn't want to go to Australia in the first place. The best bit about it all was the food and fabulous wine on Air Zealand, because I travelled first class. The hotel where I stayed was one of the best in the world, although it wasn't my sort of hotel.' Nestled between the Pacific Ocean and the sparkling Gold Coast Broadwater, and designed in partnership with the Gianni Versace fashion house, the Palazzo Versace in Brisbane is one of the world's top five-star luxury hotels. For someone accustomed to walking around in jodhpurs and mucking out stables, to find herself thrust into this world was uncomfortable for Suzi.

The couple spent three weeks in Australia. Back home, Kim Burton-Race spoke to the media. As the hounding continued, Suzi's stock phrase would become, 'There are a lot of things I could tell you, but I am not going to tell you anything. I am not here to give you a story.'

Asked what had attracted him to Suzi in the first instance, John was to tell The Guardian's Jay Raynor in April 2008, 'She is not interested in money. She's got a brain. She likes food. She likes wine. I can sit and bore the shit out of her by talking about food and wine. It's just so nice. Because she's so strong and independent, I get the feeling she doesn't need me at all. Sometimes I feel like a little boy looking for his mother's approval.'

34

JUNGLE DRUMS

IN THE process of divorce and just when he must have thought his life couldn't get any worse, Kim shut the New Angel they co-owned without his knowledge and sacked the 20-strong staff. Kim then pinned a sign on the door, which just so happened to include John's mobile telephone number so all and sundry could inquire as to what was transpiring. She wrote: 'It is with deep regret that as of Tuesday 27 November 2007 the New Angel restaurant and rooms will cease trading. Please direct all inquiries to John Burton-Race.'

The jungle drums reached John when the paparazzi photographed him as he left the jungle. He was the fourth contestant voted off by the public, following PR guru Lynne Franks. They hadn't hit it off; John found her objectionable and lazy. He had, however, found favour with the 1970s supermodel Janice Dickinson, saying she was 'bonkers and a complete mental case' but with a big heart. John did well on the show: he and Jason 'J' Brown, from the boyband Five, won six meals for the camp after taking part in the Dreadful Drop Bushtucker Trial. The pair had to climb into a wooden crate on a high wire, strung over a lake containing three floating stars. Inside the crate was a hand crank, which moved the crate across the wire. The aim of the trial was for John and J to somehow guess how far along the wire they were, and then release the bottom of the crate so they fell out into the lake. The aim was to fall through the centre of the stars. The first large star won them one meal, the second slightly smaller star won two and the third and smallest star won them three meals.

John said later he would have enjoyed remaining in the jungle longer, as it had been a great experience and a memorable time in his life—but much harder than he imagined. At first, he enjoyed the solitude and peace, but this didn't last. He had a series of arguments with Lynne Franks because of their opposing and extreme personalities. John ended up as the camp's chief cook and at one point fell foul of Janice Dickinson, who refused to eat certain types of meat, including kangaroo, crocodile and possum. He was voted off on 24 November and during his final chat with presenters Ant and Dec, he explained that as a chef, he had a very open mind when trying new types of food and that was why he disliked Dickinson's refusal.

After hearing that Kim had closed the New Angel, he tried to call the restaurant, but the phone simply rang out. He managed to make contact with the head chef, who confirmed his suspicions about what Kim had done. With Kim having posted his mobile number on the door, John was in turbulent waters. He was sinking fast, and lower than a snake's belly in a wagon wheel rut. He returned to the UK with an overdraft of £15,000, was hounded by suppliers and the Press—and hounded by his own conscience. Baton in hand, he had perfectly orchestrated his own demise. He declared himself bankrupt two months after Kim was herself made bankrupt, following an application to the High Court from a creditor owed £15,000. Kim told the Western Morning News that reports of a £3.6 million divorce settlement were ridiculous, stating that she had lost her home and was living in rented accommodation.

John's pockets suddenly felt chillingly empty. He had received £65,000 for I'm A Celebrity, but with agent fees and tax, he was left with £35,000. That didn't last long, because once back in the UK, he was instructed to liquidate all his assets for the divorce. 'I got shafted when I went to Australia, that's what happened,' he told food critic Jay Rayner in April 2008. 'There's no rationale to a woman who shuts a place down that she's drawing a salary from. I mean, I understand a woman scorned and all that, but it doesn't make sense.'

It had made perfect sense to Kim, however. Her decision was based on the realities of the business which, if truth be told, had been failing badly for some time. Having been warned in September 2006 by managers that the restaurant had little or no future, the following year it was still hanging on — purely by the amount of money passing through the till. 'This is nothing to do with my relationship with John, it's about doing the right thing in business,' Kim told The Evening Standard. 'I couldn't believe he had gone off to the jungle after leaving our family and the business in such a mess.' At the height of its fortunes, the restaurant included a cookery school and a top table service at which John acted as personal chef to private parties. According to John, Kim had always been far more ambitious materially than himself. When they met in 1996, Kim was a successful businesswoman in her own right, having built up an extremely successful bespoke travel business in which airline seats were block-booked and sold to charter operators. Avro plc had a healthy turnover of £175 million and was eventually bought by Monarch Airlines. Kim then established a property business, buying and renovating large houses. As her first marriage crumbled, she began seeing John and they married in 1997. Those first four years were bliss. It was not until 2002 when John Burton-Race at The Landmark was failing, and he accepted the Channel Four commission for French Leave that cracks appeared. When John was living a chef's life, he rose early and got home late when his family were asleep. In France, they spent more time together and John realised they had nothing in common.

Meanwhile, Suzi returned from Australia to home in Strete. She parked her car and placed Pip in his pushchair. As she was walking up the path to her cottage, she noticed a man behind her. He ran towards her, explaining he was from the Daily Mail and she would be paid £160,000 for an interview. She told him she was not interested. She told John and his response was typical Burton-Race — 'We might need that later!'

According to Martin Blunos, Kim appeared to be the only one who didn't know about the affair. Everyone was thinking, 'How is he getting away with it?' He met John at a pop-up John Burton-Race Restaurant at an Ideal Homes Show and it was clear John wasn't self-conscious about the situation. 'His attitude seemed to be, "Fuck it, it happened, it's no good dwelling on it, move on",' Martin tells me. 'John would appear to be one of those people who can constantly refresh himself and even today possibly he still feels like Mr. Teflon, where nothing sticks. Whenever we talk about his children, his love shines through. On another level, people can be with him and he can be very cold towards them. That defense mechanism will kick in, so no one sees or knows the real John Burton-Race, because he will switch character.'

It is impossible to be nice all the time; life simply isn't like that. You may not think it as we flounder under enormous piles of new cookery books year on year, but the culinary world actually is very small. Martin learnt from chef Brian Turner that you should at least try to be nice because you never know if you see them on the way up or on the way down. 'You get more out of people being nice than being an arsehole, and your blood pressure doesn't hit boiling point because you are so angry,' says Martin.

John had gone from living in a £1.5 million Georgian rectory in Ashprington to finding himself jobless and penniless. Wondering whether he would ever bounce back like a man on a white charger, his friend Clive Jacobs, the millionaire and former shareholder of lastminute.com, stepped up. In 2008 he purchased the New Angel from the receivers and re-installed John as executive chef—a role he is skeptical of, having little time for it in today's industry. He was back where he belonged and where he felt most comfortable: behind the kitchen door, salaried and back on track. But in the case of John Burton-Race, nothing is for certain. The agreement was that he would be given a salary, which certainly wasn't as much as he was used to, but he was allowed to keep external earnings from books and television appearances under a separate account. So, John kept his head below the parapet, avoiding as best as possible the inevitable fallout from the failure of his marriage and the collapse of the family business. Meanwhile, Kim gave a series of interviews with the tabloids, accusing John of drunkenness and abusive behavior, and, on one occasion, said he fired a shotgun in their house. I pressed John about this incident. In previous interviews he neither confirmed nor denied it. To set the record straight, he did.

The situation arose when he and Kim came home late after a night out to find his stepdaughter Eve and her then boyfriend with what he thought were drugs on the kitchen table. John already disliked the boy and the thought that someone had brought 'stuff' into his house produced a spark which ignited a bonfire in his mind. In a candid interview with the Evening Standard in 2007, Kim recalled: 'John had been drinking heavily and began ranting and raving. He was swearing and vowing to kill the boy. I thought he was joking but he staggered into the utility room, unlocked the gun cabinet and began loading it.' John kept a Beretta and a special edition Browning worth £7,500 locked away. Eve ushered her boyfriend out of the kitchen, and Olivia and Kim tried to wrestle the gun from John. 'He was in a really black rage,' she continued. 'Olivia was pushed to the floor and we were both hit in the face with the gun butt. Then he pulled the trigger and fired into the floor. I was terrified.' According to Kim, Eve and her boyfriend fled the house and then Kim phoned the police. When questioned later, however, Kim said there must have been a mistake. 'I shouldn't have done that, but I was very, very scared. John could have blown our heads off. He loved those guns.'

I asked John how much truth was in Kim's comments. It did happen, he says. He is reluctant to talk about it in any great detail and is certainly not proud of his actions. Afterwards he left the house in his Porsche 911 not sure of what to do and drove towards Exeter before turning around. On his way back, he was conscious of a police helicopter above. He drove on to the beach near the public toilets at Torcross and saw police cars in the area. He then drove back towards Strete, opened a gate to a field and parked his Porsche behind a wall near the King's Arms pub—a track more suited to a four-wheel-drive vehicle than a high-performance sports car. The car was lower than the wall and it couldn't be seen so John left it there, hopped over the wall and walked to Suzi's cottage. Devon and Cornwall Police later confirmed that officers attended a disturbance allegedly involving a shot gun, but no one was arrested, and no further action was taken. It is clear speaking about the incident does not sit well with John. It is something he would sooner forget.

35

KITCHEN CRIMINALS

CHEFS ARE a good commodity for television. While they are often paid very little for their expertise, they make entertaining programmes. Early on in his career in front of camera, John recognised that when producers wanted him, he had to be the entertainer or the controversial figure—when all he wanted to be was himself. He might have been a natural for television but when it came to dealing with customers, he was out of his comfort zone. He couldn't cope with having to be polite for the sake of it, and that people had seen him on television and wanted to say hello didn't sit well. He is aware this is part of the process: exceptional chefs, like rock stars, become personalities. But with it comes the burden of responsibility. However, opportunities for screen time kept coming his way. That everyone felt they knew him and slightly owned him was uncomfortable for John, so when he felt no longer prepared to play that game, others thought he wasn't very nice. For John, it was about respecting his privacy, particularly when he went about his ordinary business. But he had chosen this world and while it was not easy, he recognised that, no matter how much it met his disapproval.

The years following I'm a Celebrity saw John take part in a number of popular television shows. In 2006 he and friend Michael Caines battled in the South West of England heats of the BBC TV series Great British Menu. Their brief was to create a menu fit for a queen. 'We were punching it out between us,' says Caines. 'I had met John several times and been to his restaurant at The Landmark and he gave me some great advice about the landscape of fine dining and the situation he found himself. What I loved about John was that he went down from London to the Carved Angel and took on what was a wonderful institution and turned it into a really good restaurant. He was much more in the public eye thanks to his television series in France, and what he did at the New Angel was to give it a purpose. He was quick to catch on to the fact he had a great larder on his doorstep, and it was a key part of what he could exploit. As a result, we went head-to-head, him at the Carved Angel and me at Gidley Park. Great British Menu was good because it gave us time among all the television antics to catch up and get to know each other a bit more. It gave us a chance to bond our friendship as well as have some fun in the kitchen. John does not hold back, so you have to float like a butterfly and sting like a bee equally. We had a couple of bruising rounds and enjoyed some good banter, but overall what we had was a great friendship and a deep respect for each other. I think we played our part in it becoming an interesting series.'

Caines tells me that while John is brutally competitive, he is also the most honest and direct person. 'If he does not like you, he will tell you and I admire that openness about him. He was honest all the way through the programmes we did together. I really enjoyed my time with him, even though it was very bruising. At the end of the day I could deal with John because there was that deep-rooted respect and I was never offended because I knew he never meant any offence. We both did a goat's cheese dish. I think my lobster fricasse had the edge over his. It was very nip and tuck, and at the end of the day I think I got in on the balance of the menu.'

Inevitably there was both joy and disappointment as the two went head-to-head in the kitchen on the day before the judging panel decided who would represent their chosen area of the country. Prue Leith was joined by the highly regarded food writer and critic Matthew Fort, with renowned restaurateur

Oliver Peyton making up the trio. In a closely fought contest, John lost to Caines—who never let his friend live it down.

In 2007 John teamed up with chef Angela Hartnett for a series entitled Kitchen Criminals, which saw them scour the country in search of the nation's worst cooks and somehow turn them into kitchen heroes. The first auditions were held in Manchester, where the two were shocked to discover the state of the country's cooking skills. Could it get any worse? Was this a challenge too far? At the Birmingham auditions, one applicant's dish was spaghetti bolognese made from leftovers, and a cremated vegetable bake with black Brussels sprouts and rock-hard potatoes. The contestants then had to poach an egg and follow John's recipe for beef and ale stew. Would the final auditions in Glasgow be any worse? Mmm, an eggshell omelette with a human hair garnish did not elicit a favourable response. This was followed by John's example of creating the perfect omelette, while Angela's dish was pan-fried salmon marinated in lime and spices.

A boot camp followed in Birmingham, where each applicant was tasked to bring an example of their home cooking. With mushy peas, a fruity sauce baguette and strawberry surprise presented to them, the contestants then had to follow Angela's simple recipe for Zabaglione while trying to master John's summer salads.

Moving on to London, one hopeful brought along a turkey surprise. It was a surprise all right—the ingredient was Marmite. Contestants then had to follow John's unusual recipe for pancakes and create Angela's chicken stir-fry dish.

The programme was produced by Pat Llewellyn's company, Optomen Television, which had also made French Leave and Return Of The Chef. Critiquing Kitchen Criminals in The Financial Times, restaurant critic Jan Moir said: 'If you want to blame one single person for the ubiquity of chefs and cookery programmes on British television right now, then Pat Llewellyn is your woman. In terms of cooking stars, she is the mother hen who laid the golden egg, discovering Jamie Oliver, the Fat Ladies, Gordon Ramsay and inflicting the weirdness of John Burton-Race on an unsuspecting nation. Burton-Race and Angela Hartnett attempt to wean cack-handed members of the public off their foul attempts at making food—steak pie sandwiches, trout stuffed with cheddar cheese—and learn how to cook properly. It's like The X-Factor with more calories but less charm.'

The format was simple: the contestants were split into teams, mentored by either John or Angela, and at the end of each episode, one team member was sent home. In the first episode, the contestants had to cook mackerel with crushed new potatoes without any guidance from their mentors. John and Angela then demonstrated starters they expected their chosen protégé to cook for the food critics in a grand finale. Angela selected salmon and scallop ravioli and John a red mullet nicoise with black olive tapenade and basil oil.

In the second episode, the contestants' first task was to cook duck breast with honey and spices...unsupervised. John was disappointed when one of his best hopes messed up. Having then demonstrated the main courses the mentors expected their chosen protégé to cook for the final, Angela's team tried to master a herb-crusted rack of lamb with fennel, courgettes and confit tomatoes, while John went for chicken with morels, leeks and new potatoes.

With the remaining three contestants slowly morphing from kitchen criminals to kitchen hopefuls, next up was a chocolate mousse, again without guidance. Angela then created a blood orange jelly with Chantilly cream and biscuits and John opted for a peach gratin with almond ice cream for the puddings they expected their protégés to prepare for the judges.

By now they were down to two protégés each, and John and Angela were charged with choosing the recruit they wished to represent them. The contestants found themselves in a professional kitchen where they were expected to practice under tough conditions—nothing new for the mentors but a new and terrifying world for the amateurs. The teams then had to cook the three-course meal for three of the country's leading food critics, who had no idea that, at the start of the series, the contestants could barely boil an egg.

The series spawned a co-authored book entitled First Crack Your Egg, published by Quadrille, in which John and Angela offered the same combination of fun, easy-to-follow recipes and practical tips as the television series. As the pair noted in the introduction: 'One of our abiding principles is that good cooking begins with the simplest of recipes and the most basic of techniques, so we've started our cookery course with the humble egg. By the time you've learnt how to cook an egg properly you have acquired several fundamentals of good cooking, such as proper appreciation of your ingredients and the importance of timing. After that, you're well on your way to being able to cook.' John included a recipe for a summer salad, combining the peppery bite of watercress with the creamy acidity of young cheese, the sweetness of pear and the nutty crunch of a walnut and breadcrumb crust.

PEAR, WATERCRESS AND GOAT CHEESE SALAD
(Serves 4)

Ingredients

1 tbsp flour
1 egg
100g breadcrumbs
100g ground walnuts
4 x 100g soft goat cheese rounds
Vegetable oil or olive oil, for frying
2 small pears
Salt, pepper and sugar
50g watercress
4 tsp walnut vinaigrette

Method

1. Put the flour in a dish or on a plate. Beat the egg in a bowl. Combine the breadcrumbs and walnuts in a separate dish, stirring to mix them evenly.
2. Take a portion each of cheese and dust it in the flour so that it is evenly coated. Dip it in the beaten egg, turning so that the whole piece is covered with egg. Then place it in breadcrumbs, turning and patting the crumbs all over the cheese so that they form a crust. Repeat with the remaining cheese.
3. Warm a skillet or frying pan with a little oil. Add the cheese and cook steadily over a medium heat. When brown underneath, turn using a palette knife and cook on the other side.

4. Meanwhile, peel each pear, cut it into quarters and remove the core. Cut each quarter in half again and season with salt, pepper and sugar.

5. Heat a second skillet or frying pan with a little oil and add the pears. Cook over a medium-high heat, turning to brown on both sides.

6. Remove the caramelised pears from the pan and divide among the serving plates. Arrange the watercress on the plates.

7. Remove the cooked cheese from the pan and drain on kitchen paper. Position the cheese on top of the pears. Sprinkle the walnut vinaigrette around the edge of the plates and service.

In 2008, John followed up the book with Flavour First: How To Get The Best From The Best Ingredients, again published by Quadrille and dedicated to his late stepfather, Dennis Arthur Race. This time, John's focus was on his favourite produce: the finest fruit and vegetables, the freshest seafood and the choicest cuts of meat and poultry. Having witnessed the growth in farmers' markets through the UK, he created dishes by starting with the finest of raw ingredients. 'Fundamentally, this book is about making the most of ingredients when they are at their freshest, tastiest and cheapest,' John notes in the introduction. 'It is about appreciating fine fresh fish and good quality succulent meat. It is about identifying the best ingredients, buying them in season and transforming them into great tasting dishes. Fifty per cent of good food is about the raw ingredients. The rest is down to the recipe and skill of whoever happens to be cooking. Here I've tried to offer the enthusiastic cook a taste of my passion for good food.' Here comes that word again—passion. It has been a part of John's culinary life reaching back to his childhood in foreign climes, watching and learning from his grandmother and the family cooks, and visiting colourful markets.

Aged 52 and seemingly once again in the ascendancy, he was able to pay the £1,000 a month in child maintenance from his salary as executive chef at the Michelin-starred New Angel and travelled daily to the restaurant from the home he shared with Suzi in Strete. At 1.30am on October 30, he left the restaurant as usual in his white BMW and headed home. Police officers spotted his vehicle straddling the white lines in the middle of the road. They lost him for a short while but spotted him again at Strete, pulling into the car park of the King's Arms pub. He left the car and began walking home when the officers approached him to take a breath test. John refused and a struggle ensued. He was eventually restrained, forced to the ground and handcuffed. At the police station, he was found to be almost one-and-a-half times over the drinking and driving limit, with 57 microgrammes in 100 millilitres of breath, the limit being 35.

Before South Devon Magistrates' Court in Newton Abbot, John admitted a charge of drink-driving and resisting a police officer in the execution of his duty. His solicitor, Mark Drew, told the court how John had worked a very long day, which had included a lunchtime meeting and a busy night in the restaurant. John had drunk moderately during the day and lost track of consumption. 'He is an intelligent, articulate middle-aged man in his 50s of good character, and he could not understand why it was considered necessary to cuff him,' said Drew, as reported in the Daily Telegraph. John was fined £800 for the first charge and banned from driving for 14 months and fined £530 for resisting arrest. He was also ordered to pay £85 costs and a £15 victim surcharge. He asked to pay in instalments of £125 a month, because of his financial circumstances following his divorce. As he left court, John told waiting reporters: 'I have absolutely nothing to say. I made a mistake. I got fined.' Once again, John's performance had manifested the vagaries of the entertainment press. While he enjoyed the fame, the infamy was proving to be far more brutal.

In 2009 John appeared as a mentor on the ITV show Taste The Nation. He was a contestant on the BBC 2 show Put Your Money Where Your Mouth Is and took part in Let's Dance for Comic Relief, when he danced to Michael Jackson's Thriller. That summer, he appeared on the ITV daytime food show Daily Cook's Challenge, and he was also two years into a four-year contract as a judge on Britain's Best Dish, alongside wine expert Jilly Goolden and chef Ed Baines. It was all good fun, but he grew restless and in early 2010 decided to leave the New Angel to concentrate on TV consultancy work. Life at the restaurant in Dartmouth ticked along nicely for the first 18 months, but then John's business relationship with Clive Jacobs began to creak and there was a disagreement over finances. More sad than angry because they had known each other for years, John stepped away. As the building fell into disrepair, it was sold and renovated. Today it operates as The Angel, a relaxed fine dining restaurant focusing on local fresh ingredients—déjà vu, you might think.

36

BRAND AMBASSADOR

AFTER HIS second divorce, John looked at how much money he had in the bank and returned to France, staying in a variety of high-end establishments and studying service in the restaurants until his money dwindled. He cleared his account and used up his overdraft. A passenger on the return ferry to England even lent him £10 because he didn't have enough petrol to drive home. That French journey was a cathartic period in his shattered life, not only for his self-esteem but also as a way of re-building his love of cookery. 'There was nothing snobbish about the fact I was deliberately targeting high-end establishments such as those by Relais & Chateau, but I wanted to see how it was done by proper people,' he tells me. 'I adore France, not so much the French but the country, and despite being the laziest people in Europe, I love the mentality, and that they stick up for themselves.'

During his travels he noted how the catering industry was almost crucifying itself by applying so many restrictions on service. 'It is impossible to run a one, two or three-star restaurant on a 39-hour week, so the restaurant has to either double the team or dilute it to a team-and-a-half to make up for the time lost, and because of that, the cracks begin to show.' On another visit in 2017, John spent upwards of £11,000 visiting up to half a dozen beautiful chateaux with Suzi and Pip, and growing increasingly grumpy because he felt they offered little value to the customer 'because they are tacky, because they are run-down, because they cannot afford the renovation costs. Some big-name chefs will get their monster white elephant which has numerous stars and about the same number of customers. That doesn't fucking work. So, what do they do? They open a fast turnaround brasserie down the road which earns all their money, which then feeds the white elephant. That doesn't make any business sense, which is why I have never chosen to go down that route. It is what Raymond Blanc had done at Le Manoir when he opened Petit Blanc and look how that turned out.'

It is fair to say that John Burton-Race sacked more chefs than he ever kept because, as far as he was concerned, they were never good enough and he couldn't find the quality he so demanded. As the investment of his love, time and patience dried up, anger replaced it. He would shout and scream, and then get a bad reputation for being a tyrant and a horrible man. And he was horrible, because he was on a mission. He was constantly driven, and every single time his personal life, financial or otherwise, went wrong, his job would be good to him. He had a need to maintain control of everything around him. It was all or nothing, all of the time, and is what helped blow his marriages apart. As he grew older, he didn't become wiser. He doesn't go out of his way to be a big shot and insult people, nor does he set out deliberately to humiliate people or be obnoxious for the sake of it; as he says himself, he doesn't even think that much. Sometimes he is terribly ashamed of himself because he doesn't stop, take a breath and think—he simply jumps. He has been on that upturned boat so many times, jumping off and then scrabbling to climb on board again.

He is most definitely not the most politically correct of people. Yet however bad people said the likes of Marco Pierre White or Paul Hollihead or John Burton-Race were, it is worth remembering that their working environment has never been an office or a church. And while kitchens today work under extreme pressure in a hot and sweaty environment, it is not only about the heat, or time pressure, or the physical and mental pressure. It is all about health and hygiene, where chefs are chefs and managers are executive chefs who do not cook. John has no time for the latter, who arrive in the morning, attend a management meeting, check on the allocation for the weekly food costs, prepare the spreadsheet, then take care of the ordering, then there are the rotas, and the ten hours is gone when instead they should be imparting their knowledge on the team. 'In a five-star establishment you might get an executive chef on £120,000 a year and a head chef on £60,000. I don't want to be on £60,000 but I don't want to be an executive chef either, so what do I do?' he says. 'In this job I would like to see people like me who enjoy cooking and want to progress and change and see different things and expand their knowledge, simply get on with the job and get someone else to take care of the pen-pushing. We don't need someone in a white coat and wearing stupid trousers. We need someone who will take their tie off and get casual; someone who has been trained as a bookkeeper. You don't need a chef for that. It's just wrong.' Really, what is executive about the job? It's caked in blood and guts. Chef changes his jacket at least three times a day, working in a frantic, exciting, emotional environment with some lunatics, because they have to be loony to do it, and they cook. Then people accuse John Burton-Race of being a dinosaur because they believe he's fighting change—but he isn't. He knows one must move with the times. He knows it's possible to give people what they want and need for their insurances and health and hygiene and working practices, and he actually think it's a great idea, because he has worked in some really filthy kitchens in the past. A case in point, he tells me, was at a five-star hotel in Madrid called the Melia Castilla. He spent the morning cleaning because he didn't want to cook in the corner he was given for being European Chef of the Year. He got his friend Nigel Marriage to strip the oven out because he was not prepared to either cook on it or in it. It sounds like the kind of place with an executive chef who, according to John, are wasting their talents. 'These 50-something ECs strut around and in my opinion are laughing stocks. They think they are doing a very important job, but it's not cooking, is it? They will never have any say on what you are putting out there and ultimately if you are not involved, the standard will fall. You will only keep a standard if you are in there with it. You can't play football from the sidelines. You may be an amazing coach, but you are not going to make any difference to that match.

Ultimately, food suffers. So, I would like to see that monumental change; get a pen-pusher, half the money, and give the head chef more cash.' I doubt for one moment that Gary Jones, as Executive Head Chef at Le Manoir, would agree with these sentiments.

Outspoken John most definitely is, but according to Martin Blunos, he is a really nice man, very human, and great with kids. 'I think John wants to be liked and loved,' he says. 'He is often perceived as being standoffish but that is because he builds a protective brick wall around himself. You take all the bricks away and you get fucked over, so he kept on erecting more rows of bricks as self-protection. You do that and people think you are a cold-hearted bastard because you push people away, then you take the bricks away and say, "This is the real me". You hide behind that brick wall and you are only going to let people in that you want to.' A nice analogy.

Some say John is passionate about cooking, but he insists that it is bigger than passion—it's a calling. Sure, there are easier ways to make money, so what draws people to the industry? For a vicar, he dresses in his dog collar. That's the uniform. And he works in an amazing church. It's a calling. Cooking is the same. All of a sudden something happens, and it doesn't matter how much you earn or the hours you put in. You have this camaraderie of like-minded people with a witty and dry sense of humour because you have to be like that. If there is any sign of weakness, you are pounced on.

As far as Gary Jones is concerned, John has always been an inspirational character. 'He has always been cooking at the highest level. You always knew when you went in to one of his places that fantastic food was going to be coming out of the kitchen. There is a thing in John's eye—you don't know what is coming next. There is a little bit of zaniness and a little bit of loveliness too.'

In August 2011, John joined Adams Foods as a Brand Ambassador, with a brief to help launch and develop products for the food service division. In the same year he was also appointed Executive Development Chef for Kerrygold and Pilgrims Choice, with responsibility for developing new products for the Pilgrims Choice brand. John brought in his friend and fellow chef Stephen Humphreys as his wingman. John had taken Stephen under his wing on other consultancy work, having seen promise in the young man. Humphreys developed a passion for cooking early, having gained an apprenticeship as a commis chef at Haileybury College in Hertford Heath, Hertfordshire. 'A head chef called Mike Hodges came out of London where he had been at the Savoy for 18 years and then Lloyds of London for 16 years,' he tells me. 'I was going to go to London because I wanted to better myself when Mike took me under his wing, and we started doing competitions together.' Working for the Compass Group UK & Ireland, the UK's largest food and support services provider, they competed successfully with other chefs from across Compass, showcasing their skills and offering an insight into the exceptional standards and quality of food served daily across the business. Stephen went on to be named Ireland Junior Chef of the Year, and decided the time was right for London. He spent six months at Le Gavroche before joining Roux Fine Dining when they opened Brasserie Roux at London Heathrow's Terminal 5, where he was a sous chef. The plan was to transfer to Texas at a later stage, but he was at Heathrow for 18 months before realising that no such opportunity would materialise. In 2000 he took on a role as one of three head chefs at London's Royal Albert Hall and enjoyed a year there until Compass lost the contract.

With a compensation payment tucked in his apron, Humphreys was put in touch with an agent who in turn put him in touch with John, at that time in a consultancy role at Sanctum On The Green in Cookham. Stephen worked a few days as an agency chef, returning to the restaurant when needed. John had already employed chef James Barber to run the kitchen. When James left, John asked Humphreys to step in. 'I was aware of John's reputation,' he says. 'It was a little daunting to work alongside a celebrity chef, but it was exciting at the same time, because I knew what a godfather he was to the industry. From the outset he was brilliant, and without doubt he is an amazing chef and proved to be the perfect mentor. He always had my back and he has taught me so much; that is why I have the utmost respect for him and will not have a bad word said against him.' With John's consultancy at Sanctum On The Green coming to an end, John went in search of pastures new in London and Humphreys returned to Hertford, gaining employment in a village pub where he created an a la carte menu alongside more traditional dishes.

The pair stayed in contact and over the next few years took part in cookery demonstrations together. They also catered for private dinner parties, including for Francis Yeoh, the prominent business personality and eldest son of the late

Malaysian billionaire Yeoh Tiong Lay. Francis Yeoh had purchased a mansion near Arundel in West Sussex, and John and Stephen cooked in the old kitchen. The late Dame Anita Roddick, founder of The Body Shop, had owned the mansion previously and Humphreys remembers the house being filled with mannequins. 'I would ring the housekeeper and give her a shopping list for the dishes we were going to cook,' he says. Deliveries would arrive from all parts of the country, including live crabs. 'We would stay in a room each. One evening we cooked for a private party, and I remember Francis Yeoh's girlfriend being an opera singer. After the meal we were invited to join the Yeoh family and a few friends in the barn, where she gave us a private operatic performance, as she was practicing for an event. It was a magical evening.'

Meanwhile, both John and Stephen had the same vision — a new restaurant. They had actively sought new premises since their time together at Sanctum On The Green. Equally important to John was maintaining an income, and the work with Adams Foods was a bonus. Stephen recalls how he and John would go to the head office, where there was a small test kitchen. Required to showcase new products, the pair would cook for prospective clients using either new or existing products. It was quite a challenge, especially as there was little time to pre-plan what to make. They would normally be given the ingredients the day before. They would then sit down, work their way through them and talk about different ideas. John was the face, and he would bring Stephen along to assist him.

When John later created his ready meals business, CookedBY John Burton-Race, with the aim of selling to supermarkets, it was Stephen he turned to. John rang him out of the blue one Friday and told him he was needed in Ireland, pronto. At the time, Stephen was working full-time at a pub in Branfield and although he was able to take time away from the kitchen, he told John he could not travel until Sunday. He boarded a flight knowing he would have to hit the ground running, because the following morning he had a portfolio of dishes to cook for John. The problem was compounded by the fact that the driver meant to pick him up from the airport was not available because he had broken his arm skiing. As a result, Stephen had to catch a bus for a four-hour, heading west from Dublin to Galway. He eventually arrived in the west of Ireland and was told to wait at the bus station for collection. There was no one there. The driver showed up an hour-and-a-half later. His immediate plan was to go prep but was to be told that the kitchen had yet to be finished, and he would be taken to the premises early the next morning. So, he went to his hotel and had dinner, where he bumped into someone else from the factory where the food would be mass-produced and packaged. The building was previously run as a pub but went bankrupt. The owners then decided to turn the back room into a kitchen, where Stephen could cook the dishes for John. It was a nightmare getting all the produce in there, with Stephen only having the Monday and Tuesday morning to prep from scratch and cook the 18 dishes to John's precise recipes, all the while making sure they tasted good, before sealing them and packaging them off to Devon—where an expectant John was waiting to taste the food before giving them his seal of approval. Stephen turned all the stoves on to get the pans going, but because the kitchen was so new and had been freshly decorated, plastic started to fall off the walls from behind the units. He eventually completed his task, stacked the dishes into a large icebox and shipped them out. The dishes included prawn and chicken korma, black bean and beef, Sri Lankan curry, and three different soups. Stephen quickly came to realise that if he could achieve that amount of work in such a tight timespan, then he could face any challenge life threw at him. A short while later, the ready meals ended up on the shelves in Dunns in Ireland. While that proved successful, it was not too long afterwards that the business in Ireland, with its four directors, fell apart.

37

BOOZY HONEYMOON

JOHN MUST have wondered if anything was ever going to go right career-wise. By now he was happily married to Suzi, and they had enjoyed several holidays in France. The couple wed on August 21, 2010 and spent a somewhat boozy honeymoon in some of their favourite regions of France. 'We were smoking and drinking excessively at the time and would stop off at some grotty little bars frequented by wizened Frenchmen sitting with their fags and drinking Pastiche,' recalls Suzi. On the outskirts of Tours, they were on the lookout for somewhere to stop for a meal. 'We were driving along this straight road and were starving,' recalls Suzi. 'We stopped at this shithole farmhouse. It was a cattle farm and I remember we drove along this gravel road and it was really dusty. We parked the car and walked into what reminded me of an art deco French restaurant. It had the feel of an American drive-in from the 1950s. It would be a dump to anybody else but not to us, because we like that sort of thing.'

The huge restaurant with its impressive fireplace was virtually empty. Only two tables were occupied, one by four well-dressed French women. The sat next to a window adjacent to the fireplace. The menu, though basic, listed classic French cuisine. 'We were in the Loire Valley and the waitress asked us if we knew what traditional Rillettes were.' Like pate, they are commonly made from pork. The celebrated rillettes—and Rillons in Tours—form the main part of the meal eaten in the middle of the day, and Suzi said they would have two of them. Advised that one would be sufficient for both, Suzi insisted that they be served two as the main course. Eating andouillette was nothing new to John, who had last ordered Rillettes while in Champagne. They are certainly not to everyone's taste. The ancient French regional sausage is made from the large intestines of the pig, crisped under a grill and served with a smooth potato purée and a creamy mustard sauce. The aroma has been likened to stale urine mixed with sweet spices. 'Weirdly, the smell turns me on rather than off,' says Suzi. 'It's like a slow dance with death, with a knife and fork. John said I always pull out the simplest food on a menu, where the emphasis is on the ingredients first.' Putting any thought of elegance aside, the sausages were cooked on the grill by the table and were delicious. 'Whenever we go to France we eat in fabulous Michelin-starred restaurants and also shit ones which cost a fortune, but the restaurants we remember most of all are the ones such as where we enjoyed the andouillette because they are so special,' Suzi tells me.

By about 4pm everyone else has left the restaurant and the owner sat with John and Suzi, a bottle of wine to hand. John ordered another bottle and Suzi reminded him that he was driving. John told his wife to shut up as he re-filled the owner's glass. John told him how amazing the andouillette was, and the owner grew emotional, saying John was just the type of person he would want to sell his farm, restaurant and cattle herd to, because he was not making money. John said he had no money to buy but the owner replied that while it was cheap, he could make it even cheaper. John said he may have a fancy car, but he and Suzi didn't have anywhere to live. 'Buy here and you will have, in France, and it will only cost you £160,000,' said the owner. I can see John's eyes clouding over as he recalls the conversation and wonders why he did not pursue the offer. 'Why aren't we there?' he asks Suzi. 'You're not there because you didn't meet me early enough,' she replies. 'You should have met me before you met the second one!'

Back in 2005, they'd found themselves in France when John accepted a consultancy role in the Cognac region. John and Suzi enjoyed walking around the old town's narrow streets of medieval timber-framed properties, and the garden mansions of wealthy merchants. John had been booked into a hotel within spitting distance of the ramparts. 'What a shithole it was,' he tells me. 'I thought, if you are going to put me up somewhere like this, I am not going to work for you because you can't be very good. I was driving a Porsche Cayman at the time, and Suzi said are we having a holiday or not? She suggested that we go to Barcelona and I thought it couldn't be more than 1,000 fucking miles, so I thought we would stop at Carcassone and enjoy a cassoulet.' From Barcelona, they headed back along the Cote d'Azur and up a zigzagging mountain road to Peillon, the jewel in the crown of the Nice hinterland. The couple looked down on the spread of Monte Carlo and saw a board advertising the Auberge de la Madone, where they sat on the terrace and enjoyed sipping champagne. 'It was really shabby but lovely. Americans would hate it,' says Suzi.

As they had no destination in mind, it was the perfect place to relax and take in the beautiful scenery … until the resident bull terrier arrived with fleas. Suzi was bitten on the ankle and began itching immediately. If John noticed, he made no comment. His head was in the handwritten wine list, which was like a bible to him. 'I thought that these people did not know what they had got, because the prices were in no way right for the labels,' says John. 'I decided to pick out several bottles because I didn't know when we would be back here again. Suzi went to itch her bite and when she came back, I told her we were going to stay. We got a room. It was lovely, with a small balcony. We could hear the crickets and see Monte Carlo below. In the evening we walked downstairs, and it was like being in a French person's house, it had that feel about it. The restaurant had been owned and run by the same family for three generations. They had lit a fire and it was if we had been transported to the 18th century. It was magical.' John and Suzi sat at a small, round table covered in handmade lace and laid with silver cutlery. They began the evening with an Edmond Briottet chestnut liqueur, which was both 'fresh tasting and utterly delectable', followed by amazing meal. They were away for two weeks, says John, but it took three months to recover from the money they spent enjoying the good life.

38

THE JOHN BURTON-RACE EXPERIENCE

IN SOUTH Africa, with its plentiful natural bounty and internationally acclaimed wines, there is little wonder that food festivals have grown in popularity. In October 2013, John was invited to attend the Delicious Festival in Johannesburg. Headlining the music was Jamiroquai, supported by a host of top South African artists including Lira, Danny K, Khuli Chana, Prime Circle and Mi Casa.

The idea was for three international pop-up restaurants — The John Burton-Race Experience, San Carlo Cicchetti and Randall & Aubin — to provide patrons with fine cuisine first-hand from John, Ed Baines and Aldo Zilley while enjoying live music from a raised vantage point overlooking the crowd. The restaurants would take limited bookings daily for lunch and dinner sittings, supported by a large artisan food market showcasing an array of African, European and pan-Asian cuisine. A music festival for food lovers and a food festival for music lovers, whichever way you flip it, it was anticipated that Delicious would take the South African entertainment and culinary world by storm

John, Ed and Aldo each took a head chef with them. and Stephen Humphreys was John's choice. This was the time when John was heading up Sanctum On The Green, as well as his restaurant in London. The pair soon got to work on the menus, initially over the phone. The plan was to send a shopping list and menus to Pete Goffe-Wood, judge of the television series MasterChef in South Africa, and John would be given a team for food prep, prior to his and Stephen's arrival. The three pop-ups were each charged with 250 elaborate covers for lunch and the same number for dinner, all prepared in a large tent under the intense African sun and in front of gas stoves that melted foreheads. John had dishes you would expect to find on a Michelin-starred menu: a venison carpaccio, sea bass with peanut rice, tempura prawn with Thai seven spice and mushroom sauce made from the shells of the prawns — all very fancy on the plate. This was followed by chocolate mousse layered like a Jaffa cake with orange ice cream. It was fabulous but ridiculously tough, particularly as they had a four-burner gas stove, the sort normally taken on a camping holiday. Then there was the small fryer, a hot cupboard with three shelves and a three-shelf oven … to do 500 covers a day, plus the prep. It was a challenge all right.

John and Stephen were in the country for five days. Friday night was set aside for Press engagements, followed by the festival itself on the Saturday and Sunday, plus a day at each end. The sun was shining, the hotel was lovely, and they enjoyed a dip in the swimming pool and felt among the privileged few as they were chauffeured to and from the event. While John was being interviewed on the radio on the Friday, Stephen went to the site to ensure everything was as it should be. He'd been promised that everything would be ready for him, even down to the desserts having been delicately cut into finger portions. All he and John would have to do was walk inside the tent to their designated workstation, plate up, and they would be good to go. When Stephen arrived, the team was just putting the chicken stock on — the very first job during prep. They had done absolutely nothing else. In only three hours, they were expected to serve the Press corps.

Stephen telephoned John, who in turn had a major dispute with the organiser, who then quit, resulting in Stephen having to cajole John into apologising to him, or the whole festival would come tumbling down. In the end he relented, but not before he vented his fury at anyone who dared come near.

Heads down, he and Stephen managed to get things moving. They were supposed to showcase everything but instead had to get something ready for only 20 people. Jamiroquai then chose to fly in by helicopter just as service began. There was dust everywhere. Even lead singer Jay Kay had to wait until the cloud of hot earth had settled before he could venture out. Once on stage, he announced to the crowd that if they wanted to eat, they should go along to his mate John Burton-Race. Everyone then descended on the pop-up. All went swimmingly, but on the second evening everything had to be prepared by candlelight; the organisers had to turn all the lights off during prep because of a power cut. With no storage available, the chefs had to try and freeze everything with dry ice. While Ed Baines relaxed during the afternoon by the hotel pool, John and Stephen ran around like headless chickens. Despite all the frustration and commotion, the organisers had expected Michelin-starred food from a Michelin starred chef—and that is exactly what they got. The event was such a success that the festival returned the following May in Johannesburg and Cape Town in December, and again in 2015.

'The thing I love about John is that in whatever restaurant he is working or at whatever event he is at, you know you are going to get blood and sweat from him,' Martin Blunos tells me. 'He will always be the first in and the last out the door. That's the measure of how committed and passionate he is. He is nothing short of a legend in the culinary world.'

39

OGGYS IN ITALY

BEING ON the road for competitions, masterclasses and demonstrations was fun but hard work and relentless, though John remained sanguine about the opportunities that came his way. 'When I was involved in doing loads of demonstrations at places like the NEC in Birmingham and London's ExCel, I would look out at the audience and think how terrifying it was, but then I would switch on and say to myself, "I know more about this than you do about my job so I am going to go out there and show off and be funny and take the mickey and make it look easy and cook while I'm talking and make jokes and have fun", because I like that interaction for the simple reason that it is scary—but that is when I come into my own.'

Even the Italian Tourist Board got in on the act in the winter of 2013, when John joined three fellow Michelin-starred chefs from France, Italy and Germany to individually design a handheld snack. Each chef was challenged to design a dish that was elegant enough to be eaten après ski with a glass of wine. The stipulation was that the snack also had to be stable enough to be carried in a rucksack up the slopes. John got together with Stephen

Humphreys, with the aim of creating a Cornish pasty but made in Devon. Once the competition was over, the plan was for the pair to enjoy a week's skiing in Alta Badia in the Dolomites. They landed in Milan, expecting to be greeted by a chauffeur, but there was no one there. They contacted the organisers and were told to get a hire car and make their own way to the resort. They exited the airport and made it to the motorway when the sat-nav packed up. With every road looking exactly the same, they ended up in the centre of Milan during Friday afternoon rush hour. They eventually made it back to the motorway and stopped at a petrol station with the intention of buying a road map but the only one they could find had a bunch of cartoon images. By the time they arrived at the beginning of the mountain stage of the drive it was dark, and once again they went in the wrong direction. It was now 10pm, six hours after they had landed.

They spotted a bar and went in, but no one spoke English, and they were all drunk anyway. One of the regulars climbed into his car, reversed into a wall and drove off. Eventually the barman came to their rescue and with very rough directions to hand, they were on their way again — just as it began to snow. Soon they came across a snow plough heading towards them. The driver told them to turn around because the road was becoming impassable. With his heart in his mouth, John carried on driving ... well, skidding mostly; it was time to put chains on the tyres. As Stephen attempted that the task, John slowly rolled the car backwards. 'The snow was getting heavier and as we drove over this mountain, suddenly there was complete darkness,' remembers Stephen. 'We carried on really slowly, and the car was simply sliding. I was really scared at this point. I told John we should pull over and he said if we did that, we were finished. Then we saw a sign warning about avalanches. I was ready to text my mum and say goodbye! John saved my life because if we had stopped and got stranded, we would no doubt have died of hypothermia.'

As the pair drove over a crest, they saw the lights of two small towns. It was 4am and they had been on the road for hours. John could not figure out why no one had reported them missing, or why no one had organised a search party. Instead, upon arrival at their hotel, they found an envelope sellotaped to the wall with John's name on it and a key card inside. Tired and fraught, they managed to snatch half an hour's sleep before meeting with two members of the tourist board. John let them know how unhappy he was with the situation, saying he and Stephen would carry on with the event and then catch the first plane out.

Each chef was given his own mountain restaurant to create the chosen dish. They had a day to prep before everyone got together to taste the snacks and enjoy a party. The European Press was out in force. While the other chefs prepared fairly simple salad boxes with dressings, John and Stephen prepared a silver platter of tiddy oggys, a traditional Devon pasty, so named as 'tiddy' means potato and 'oggy' means pasty. The pair made their own pastry out of lard and horseradish and used Italian pork for the fat content. The oggys went down a storm and made the cover of EasyJet magazine. They missed out on five days' skiing, but it was an experience neither would have given up. 'Rather than John Burton-Race and his head chef, we were two friends in Italy driving through a snowstorm! Experiences like that made our relationship so special. We would do anything for each other,' says Stephen. With the competition over, they drove to Genoa, the nearest airport to the resort ... which is where they should have flown to in the first place.

OGGIES
(Serves 8)

Ingredients

(PASTRY)
375g plan flour
15g salt
125g unsalted butter, cut into dice
125g lard, cut into dice
1 egg, beaten
60ml cold water

(FILLING)
450g topside of beef, cut into small pieces

1 onion, dived into 1cm cubes

200g potato, peeled and diced into 1cm cubes

1 carrot, peeled and diced into 1cm cubes

1 turnip, peeled and diced into 1cm cubes

Salt and freshly milled black pepper

15g parsley, chopped

1 tsp Worcestershire sauce

1 egg, beaten

Method

1. Sieve the flour and salt into a large bowl. Add the butter and lard and rub them into the flour until the mixture resembles bread-crumbs. Add the beaten egg and pour in the water. Gently bind the pastry together and press it into a ball. Wrap in cling film and refrigerate for at least 2 hours.

2. Put the meat into a bowl. Add the onion, potato, carrot and turnip, stir together and season with salt and lots of pepper. Add the parsley and the Worcestershire sauce, and stir everything together.

3. Cut the pastry in half and roll it out. Cut out 8 circles about 16cm in diameter. Brush around the edges of each circle with the beaten egg. Divide the filling into 8 and spread it in a line across the centre of each circle of pastry. Fold the pastry over the filling so that the two sides meet. Using your thumb and forefinger, squeeze the pastry together to seal and crimp the edges. Brush the tops with the remaining egg wash and make small holes in the tops to allow the steam to escape.

4. Cook them in an oven preheated to 200°C/400°F/Gas 6 for about 25 minutes. Lower the oven temperature to 180°C/350°F/Gas 4 and cook for a further 25 minutes. Serve hot.

40

THE INEVITABLE BURNOUT

I N 2014 a new opportunity presented itself in London's Notting Hill. John had been in discussions with the Russian owner of a Georgian restaurant and, having taken the decision to step in with his expertise, was handed a tiny budget to work with. He was tasked buying any necessary equipment as quickly and cheaply as possible to get the restaurant up and running. John concentrated on the kitchen design and Stephen Humphreys came on board as his second in command, responsible for key administrative areas such as health and safety, as well as organising staff training. Slowly but surely, the restaurant—previously off-radar apart from occasional Eastern Europeans who frequented the place—was transformed and rebranded The Angel. It was closed on Sundays and Mondays, so John made the weekly drive from Devon and return home after service around 11pm on the Saturday night, having done 80 covers. He would always be first in the kitchen, normally having put in a good one-and-a-half hours before Stephen's arrival at 7.30am. He would work religiously, his creativity firing on all cylinders, and as a result the restaurant was an instant success, though it took its toll on John. Slaving away in a basement kitchen with a couple of stoves, a freezer and other machinery and no windows, it was tiny, hot and sweaty. The team was new. They would come, then leave or walk out, which all added to the stress. The Russian owner was proud of the result and was busy conjuring up grand plans to open a restaurant in Moscow. As far as John was concerned, it was always another day at the office, conscious that his pay cheques came from different countries every month. But he did not give a monkey's as long as he was paid.

The reviews were plentiful and favourable. 'I have rarely found such superior food, service and ambience in one location' noted Square Meal. London Dining Reviews said: 'This new clearly Michelin level dining venue in Notting Hill is surely to become a firm favourite with locals and those looking for an excellent and good value dining experience. It's finding its feet at the moment, but staff are helpful, it's suitable for walk-ins and you won't find much better food in many London eateries, bar the critic's favourites. This should well and truly be a contender for one of the best new openings.' And Laurent Perrier noted: 'As for John Burton Race, his cooking has a classic sense of sophistication in the type of space that will no doubt see the Michelin men giving him their approval in the not-too-distant future.'

The first period of opening possibly cost the restaurant its Michelin star. Despite the creation of amazing food, John found it hard to create regular custom during the week in this part of London. The restaurant was just around the corner from the Ledbury, where Stephen Humphreys took the opportunity to pop in and speak to the head chef. For the first four or five years, they had no one in for lunch either. Then, when people found it, the restaurant grew to become the fifteenth most popular in the world. With that in mind, John and Stephen pressed on, conscious that the Russian owner, who held the lease to the building, had possibly pushed them to open too quickly. Despite initial setbacks, the restaurant picked up three rosettes, the most a venue can gain in its first year. The judge informed John that he had enjoyed the best meal in London that year. With the food typically presented beautifully and tasting delicious, the menu changed on a regular basis, even from lunch to dinner, depending on John's constant creativity and stream of food consciousness.

Stephen remembers there being three kitchen porters, two on larder and one on pastry. There was someone on fish and a sous chef alongside Stephen and

John, all cramped in that tiny kitchen, serving up ridiculously splendid food. Working such long hours and a weekly commute from Devon, it was inevitable John's health would suffer. One particular evening he and Stephen had decided to enjoy a Chinese meal together in the Queensway. John collapsed in the street and the next thing he knew he was in Brompton Hospital with a heart condition and stomach ulcers. Years of a manic lifestyle, chain smoking and bingeing on caffeine and sleeping three hours a night caught up with him.

Recuperating in Devon, the stress over lack of money continued to haunt him. Attending a dinner for the local hunting fraternity with Suzi at a hotel near Dartmouth, he had just begun the meal when he collapsed, this time waking up in an ambulance. He had suffered a ruptured ulcer, which led to sepsis. He underwent emergency surgery, during which it was discovered that the sepsis had damaged his colon and bowel. In recovery, he was devastated to find out he had been fitted with a temporary stoma bag. Keyhole surgery followed to remove four abscesses, and John was left feeling like a pincushion. His potassium levels went through the roof, resulting in the destruction of some of his heart muscle and one of his ventricles. Back at Brompton Hospital, further investigations revealed he was suffering from blood flow issues to the brain. With one side of his heart destroyed, stents were fitted to the side of his neck to aid blood flow. It was 18 months before he was fully fit again. Ever stoic, he battled through and returned to The Angel when he was well enough, conscious that he had a restaurant to run and money to earn for his family.

Approaching the end of 2015, and with the restaurant rightly earning a name for itself in all the right circles, the Russian owners were conscious that their five-year lease on the property was due to expire. With things very much up in the air, Stephen went to Copenhagen for a short break and a four-month long position in the kitchen at the prestigious Noma. He was one of only a dozen chefs selected to work there out of 2,000 applicants. 'John was really happy for me because it was his name that got me in there in the first place,' he tells me. He had impressed sufficiently to be offered a full-time position, and while the experience was so different to anything he had done so far, he wanted to use it in his own cooking. It was while he was in Copenhagen that the Russian owner of The Angel left the country.

It came as a complete shock to John. 'No one likes to admit, "I can't do that anymore". It still upsets me even now,' he says. 'I definitely had it in my mind that I wouldn't be able to work again, but that actually inspired me to keep going. While I worked my 14-hour days, and although I struggled with it, I could in a way forget about it, as I was able to concentrate on my work in the kitchen. I couldn't imagine sitting at home and thinking about all the shit that was happening to me in a physical way. Most of my dreams are based on the thoughts of a 12-year-old.' During this time, culinary plaudits continued to rain on The Angel. It achieved a place in Harden's Top 10 new openings in 2015, followed by three AA Rosettes and a slot in Open Table's Top 100 restaurants.

With the owner out of the country, John was left with a list of angry unpaid suppliers. He tracked down the owner's wife, who was still living in in a gated property with electric fencing and security cameras in Virginia Water. John explained that even though he knew the restaurant had closed, he still wanted to be paid and he also wanted the suppliers to be paid, because that's what happened in England. They met in a small coffee shop in a square in Virginia Water, where John was handed a cheque and a bonus in cash, and that was that.

Once more at home in Devon, in 2016 John had plenty of time of time to ponder his future. It was 18 months of a sedentary lifestyle, remaining incommunicado, piling on weight and growing more depressed. He needed to lose weight and was happy to give up everything except red wine and beer.

With decades of experience to lean on, he formulated a new business venture with friend Chris Sherville, called Two Grumpy Chefs. The aim was simple: to curate parties from the intimate to the outrageous. They would provide menus, wine and support staff tailored to the client's taste. 'It all came from me sitting at home and thinking what we could do together,' John tells me. 'We did a couple of jobs. I was doing all the cooking and Chris was doing the shopping.' They did a couple of jobs, but it was something of nothing really, and in the end, John told Chris he did not want to bother with it. There was, however, one very humbling experience to come from the enterprise. 'There was this lovely woman in Dartmouth, and we prepared a dinner party for her husband,' he tells me. 'She ended up spending a lot of money, and she then told me that I had cooked her husband his last supper. He had been a magistrate and was suffering from incurable cancer, and I felt really guilty giving her a bill. His request had been that I would cook his last meal when he could actually digest food. It was a huge compliment. He remembered how I used to cook for him when I had been at L'Ortolan. The couple had retired and moved to some fairly remote location in Devon.' John cooked in an annexe to the main property. 'I chatted with him and he knew all the dishes I used to do but I didn't do any more because I called it old fashioned, and he called it amazing. He reminded me of the things I had done at L'Ortolan that I had forgotten about. I made up a menu based upon a reasonable balance, although there must have been five to six thousand calories in each of the courses. He then called me in after the meal and opened a very expensive bottle of red wine. We drank together, and then his wife told me the next day that they would love to have me back, but it would probably be just her, and then he passed away. She told me she had loved the dining experience because she had never dreamt of getting John Burton-Race to go to their house to cook. The couple just happened to come across the Two Grumpy Chefs link on a website and immediately thought that it could not it be the same John Burton-Race. I didn't know what to charge because I was just thinking about my next job, and she said she would have paid anything for it because it was her husband's dying wish. For me to cook his last supper brought everything into perspective, and I felt very humbled. You cannot get more emotional than that.'

That is not entirely true: John Burton-Race does get emotional. Get him talking about food and you can see it in his eyes and hear it in his voice. When we met that first time in Torquay, he had just put in a 70-hour week. He told me then that he would probably die under a stove in a kitchen goodness knows where, because he was privileged to be involved in what he really loved. That driving force was almost the end of him. For almost two years he was out of the limelight, dealing with a succession of serious illnesses. At one stage he was advised by doctors to never work again. His life, like his career, has been one hell of a roller-coaster ride, and even today he does not seem overly bothered about planning for the future. He never thinks about tomorrow, but knows that if he stops working, his family does not eat.

He once commented that if he had chosen a different career, then it would have been a painter. 'There are perhaps only two or three services throughout my career where every single thing that went out of the kitchen, to me was like a Picasso; three times that I didn't need to seek anyone else's approval.' One of those times was at L'Ortolan, another when he was in Barbados and the third time in London. 'Even as a young chef, if I went to speak to a customer who had complimented me on the food, I would look straight through them. I would know what table they were on and I would know what I had sent out, but I would also know that it hadn't been perfect. I would think, "You don't know what you are talking about. You are telling me how brilliant I am, but it was shit". Marco (Pierre White) would no doubt say, "Just say it like it is", but that obviously gives off a bad impression because the customer would think you were even more bonkers than they had thought you were originally. Sometimes I would agree and tell a lie, by just saying a simple thank-you. Sometimes I would say I was really pleased that they were pleased but that I could do better, and then walk back to the kitchen.'

I ask John whether he has read Anthony Bourdain's seminal work Kitchen Confidential: Adventures In The Culinary Underbelly. He has, as no doubt has every other notable chef in the country. The book was an eye-opener to some of the industry's challenges and inspired many to pursue a career in food. Many chefs have endured a life like Bourdain's, whose tragic death revealed a deeply troubled alcoholic dependency with a history of substance abuse. Many might believe that it is easy to be an alcoholic if you work in the catering industry and your ability to get through the day in a pressured environment is solely reliant on drink or drugs, but then that is no life. First published in 2000, at a time when John was creating his own waves at John Burton-Race at The Landmark, Kitchen Confidential was a particularly revealing book. Like many of his contemporaries, John Burton-Race has been cooking at that elevated level throughout his career, and while he clearly enjoys a drink, he is not an alcoholic and has never taken drugs. He is the first to recognise that his can be a brutal industry, one with a serious impact on personal lives. He learnt very quickly that when you are in a position of ownership, there is a fine line between success and failure, and you cannot afford to take time off when you like. First in, last out, seven days a week. That's the bottom line — the only line. Kitchen Confidential and Anthony Bourdain are testament to the fragility of the industry.

John Burton-Race's contribution to the British culinary world should never be overlooked. 'The heyday may have gone, and while I am not suggesting that his days are less fruitful, sometimes we are men of the moment and we do not appreciate it,' says Gary Jones. 'John is significant in what he has done, in that he helped push forward British food and gave other people platforms to work. He has had many chefs through his kitchen who have gone on to do great things, and he continues to contribute to the culinary world in the southwest. He is a fighter, he doesn't give up, he is controversial — but then that is good because it makes him interesting. He is outspoken so he is worthy of being listened to, but there is also a great depth of knowledge. I know that part of John's problem is within his personality. Even though he seems confident, he is not. There is self-doubt and he has struggled with certain things in his life, and that side of him is not generally known. Some of the things he has done may have been thought of as him being difficult when, in fact, he is actually quite shy. He sees it as it is and doesn't want to waste time with people. Why bother, he thinks, and I quite admire that in him. Why should you have to stand on ceremony? You go to lots of restaurants and you don't expect to see the owner. It is sometimes nice to have someone like John to remind us that maybe that isn't important. I hope he continues to be a culinary influence. He is tenacious, and I wish him well as I know he has had a difficult time of late and to be honest I think he deserves better.'

In a way John Burton-Race has been a victim of his own circumstance. He will be the first to say there have been times when he has gone into business with somebody and a problem has manifested itself, which then has exploded into a massive fallout. Whether those situations have been down to bad luck or a bad judgement call is anyone's guess. 'He would do absolutely anything for his friends,' says Stephen Humphreys. 'While he is a very clever guy, even behind the scenes we have had a lot of laughs. All the bad press, you don't see any of that. In a restaurant with service there is pressure, and it is the same in any kitchen. It is never personal with John. All he has ever tried to do is deliver the best food possible for the customer. If he took things personally, he would never have survived. I don't recall ever having fallen out with him. He is just a lovely guy. In my eyes he is like the godfather of cooking.'

Single-minded and clearly opinionated, if John did not like something, he would say so and be done with it. You would be hard pushed to find a grey area, because everything is either black or white. He was like that with television, where he reached the stage of not enjoying it any more. While he loved all the showing off, opportunities got sillier and sillier, which is how he was to lose faith with his (then) agent. 'I had been asked to do some stupid programme after I had already done one for Channel 5 which had nothing to do with food. It was called Super Bra and was all about hair and beauty. Because I was successful at that, my agent asked me to do another programme but she didn't like my declining it, having set the whole thing up. To be fair to her, I was trouble. I wouldn't say yes, and I wasn't politically correct. Basically, I was a naughty boy in that I would tell people to get stuffed if I didn't like doing something, and all of that catches up with you. It wasn't a question of me showing off, I was simply coping. It is silly because as any celebrity chef knows, we are in the limelight, but sometimes I just want to keep people away. It isn't a question of me being the big I am, it is more a case of, "Please leave me alone because I want to be quiet".'

John tells me about the time he was walking towards Harrods after he'd appeared on I'm A Celebrity and a lorry driver beeped him. Then a taxi driver let out a passenger who asked John to sign a piece of paper for his wife. 'It's nice, to a point. I am not moaning about it, because from the limelight comes monetary reward, but some people, like myself, find it difficult to cope with. Nearly everyone I know has been divorced. It is almost a part of life. Some of the stuff I have had to deal with in my life has been horrendous, but I am not too worried about any of that because I am lucky that I manage to stay true to what I believe in. I can do the job; I love it and even at my age I am still learning. It is an amazing thing and I have met some wonderful people, although I get fed up with those who tell me sometimes that they want quality but won't pay for it. If you want a beautiful restaurant with beautiful food, it costs a lot of money. I know it is easier to have a lesser standard and drive a lesser car, but is it the same as the real thing?'

41

BOUNCING BACK

JOHN HAS always been in charge of his own destiny. Having kicked his heels for 18 months due to his catalogue of illnesses and near-death experiences, he was desperate for the sanctuary of the kitchen; somewhere he could re-establish his own boundaries. You might think John has made life difficult for himself by living the past few years in the southwest of the country, where produce is bountiful, but opportunities are few. He works in an industry that is quite relentless and extremely unforgiving. Like the bus analogy, it is easy to catch a ride, but once you get off, it is hard to get back on again. It's that treadmill effect, where you get conditioned to the pace, but treading the line is difficult as you try to make the most of the conditions you have in front of you.

The year 2018 ushered in a new chapter in John's life at The Grosvenor Hotel in Torquay, owned by The Richardson Group Ltd. The hotel was to undergo a facelift and John Burton-Race was to have his own restaurant. He became involved in the kitchen design, as well as menu planning and food preparation. With so much commitment and passion continuing to flow through that battered body, it is easy to imagine that those days of blood, sweat and tears, those days of first-in, last-out would manifest themselves once again. In a candid Guardian interview with Rachel Cooke back in 2005, John said: 'Some chefs on TV, I wouldn't give them a job as a commis. They haven't seen a kitchen for years. I've watched all these chefs shoot up to the skies like rockets on Guy Fawkes Night, explode in a ray of colour, then go bankrupt and disappear.' Well, he hadn't seen a kitchen in almost two years. He had lit up the skies with his superlative cuisine and he had most certainly gone to hell and back, but John had definitely not disappeared. You can never keep a good man down. He would have his own kitchen, with his own staff and his own name over the door. He was back where he belonged.

At 60 years of age, his name was once again up in lights, staring out in all its lavishness from a new signboard for all the world to see. Walking through the doors of the hotel in fresh whites, he felt empowered once more; one of the true edifices of culinary expertise was fired up and raring to go. Yes, we have been here before, a number of times, but here he is, back in the present tense, where he wants to be local, where he can go home at night to be with his wife and son and play the family man. 'This is Devon, and there are not that many super jobs out there that will pay the money. That is a fact of life, which is hard to swallow,' he tells me. He has not forgotten what it was like to be completely skint and had even thought of returning to London or travelling abroad to realise the income that runs parallel with the prestige of a top job. But then, he also appreciated the reality of his situation, having come out of hibernation after 18 months. He knuckled down and despite everything seemingly mismatched, he created a brand new kitchen and built up a fabulous team of willing workers keen to learn from him. He could cook exactly what he wanted, all the time hoping that a certain Keith Richardson of the Richardson Group would realise the potential in what he had created. But at the back of his mind was the nagging doubt of exactly how long he could continue waiting for the turnaround in a business to make financial sense. Richardson told him to concentrate on the food and everything else would take care of itself. But it did not. Sometimes life throws a curve ball and my word, has John Burton-Race had to suffer more than his fair share of those. He worked his socks off to get the restaurant exactly how he wanted it, and then Keith Richardson moved him to the Grand Hotel with the grand idea for John to replicate the theme. It was not to be. He knew what he had wanted to achieve, but he also knew he could not get the quality he wanted because the money was not available to him. As a result, he was learning how to compromise; something he had never had to do before. He also realised that the older he became, the fewer jobs and money there were. He also knew from past experience that people were reluctant to pay for experience, because there had been lots of situations that had shaken his confidence and self-esteem over a long period of time. It's a bit like the old trooper who keeps getting knocked down and eventually thinks to himself, 'I am just tired.' But no, wait, this is John Burton-Race. He is most definitely not fed up or tired of his work—because he can jump in and hide in the kitchen where he is a chef again and he can go and be true to himself and show off. That's more like it.

With the John Burton-Race Hotel and Restaurant up and running, John agreed to the move to The Grand with the intention of re-creating his own brand of culinary magic. He admits he is a dreamer because all too often it's the only way he has been able to deal with certain situations. 'I love cooking, am passionately driven by it and always learning something from it. I am lucky where I have a job in which I can become totally absorbed in it,' he says. And he did for a while, but then the cracks began to show, both in his relationship with Richardson and his own conscience. Then the hotel group found itself in administration. Back at the John Burton-Race Hotel and Restaurant, bookings for dinner and weddings and private parties were pulled because the organisers of those parties suddenly had cold feet, not really knowing what administration meant. For John there were still bills to pay, and he'd spent months slaving over a hot stove, creating menus and memories... for what exactly? Slowly the reality dawned on the dreamer, and he came to a grand awakening. He was floundering by that damned upturned boat. Time to bail out. So, he quit. Today, in hindsight, he knows going into business with the group was a mistake. He lost out big time financially. It was time to move on, both financially and for his own peace of mind. It was easier to walk... back to his rented farmhouse amid Devon's idyllic countryside, away from prying eyes, back to the cocoon of his family with the dogs and horses and chickens and hens and geese and goodness knows what else. Seated in the kitchen, surrounded by cookbooks and piles of Horse & Hound magazines on the kitchen table, we drink coffee from assorted crockery as mismatched as his life. We talk about food and what he enjoys cooking and how he enjoys experimenting with recipes. His eyes light up and the enthusiasm for the subject matter simply pours forth. If Suzi decides to cook Sunday lunch, John will take over, so she doesn't bother any more. Leave it to the master. His religion is his kitchen. 'Time management is key, balancing cooking with the media and the day-to-day running of a business, which requires you to be in or out of your comfort zone. When I had my restaurants, I would like to get up in the morning and be creative and think about a dish but in reality, that became a rarity. The week was normally structured around the daily elements of routine and within the constraints of service time. The managing of the diary was key, and the use of my time was key. When you are away from the restaurant you have to plan for your absences. It is all down to the disciplines and structures that you put in, in order for you to survive. I look at what it took to create such places as Le Manoir and that helped me in my understanding of running a business. In this industry it is difficult to manage time, so you have to be quite selfish about it.'

There have been lots of situations in his life where if he had approached situations in a different way, then the end results may have panned out better. In hindsight, perhaps his decision to head to the jungle in I'm A Celebrity while all hell was breaking loose at home could be seen as more an act of desperation than a strategically important move, but then he has enjoyed more successes than failures through his television work. Such appearances help amplify what a chef does, because it is what they do that matters. For John, if he keeps cooking and maintains his skillset at a certain level, he stands a chance of always being relevant—simply because when he cooks, he cooks brilliant food, and that is all that really matters in this game. Throughout his career, no doubt uppermost in his mind will have been the thought, 'Do people come to my restaurant and enjoy what they eat?' If they do, then no, he may not be so trendy any more, or the flavour of the month, and he might even be on the back burner, but it does not mean that he cannot be successful, because as a chef, ultimately, you are trying to please yourself. If you achieve that, then the diners will keep oncoming. And he knows that, as does every chef worth his or her salt.

42

THE EVER-EVOLVING JOURNEY

THANKS TO a constantly evolving style, John Burton-Race held two Michelin stars across three restaurants for 17 years. For that he not only juggled technical expertise with a high level of consistency, but also reached beyond technique, drawing on the influences that so inspired him during that time, and willingly passing those skills on to young brigades eager to feed off his knowledge. His has been an extraordinary, evolving journey; from those childhood days in the Far East to a working chef in London where he endured long days and nights which were both physically and mentally draining, when he would taste food all day and become sick of it, only to stop off for a kebab on the way back to his grotty flat. He tells me that one of the best meals he ever ate was a 13-course Asian banquet in Singapore. A far cry from today's passion for fish and chips by the sea or a Sunday joint of roast rib or sirloin of beef with roast potatoes, Yorkshire pudding and vegetables.

He knows full well that with any chef, you are only ever as good as your last meal. That thought probably lingered while he was in the jungle when he had to prepare possum for the I'm A Celebrity camp. He lived on an average of 300 calories a day and lost two stone in weight in three weeks, but he still could not stomach the thought of eating too much possum, as to him it felt like he was eating a rat and he had nothing with which to disguise the flavour.

I ask Michel Roux Senior what advice he would offer today's aspiring young chefs, and he tells me: 'Do not try to run before you know how to walk. Take your time, and if you work somewhere and the chef is a good chef—and I am talking about any level, whether it be one star or no star—swallow your pride because you are not there to show that you are better than him or her, you are there to learn. It is very difficult to help someone when it is a question of mentoring. If you cannot control yourself, then you cannot help others. With John, I am a strong believer that he has grown out of his problems from his earlier days and I believe he can train people and offer a good example. He has learned by his mistakes and now I hope he is in a better place. Even the people around him will sense a better spirit.'

You might think that today John Burton-Race has plenty of time on his hands, but the work keeps rolling his way. It was not long after leaving his position with the Richardson Group that he took up a temporary position heading the kitchen at Devon's Millbrook Inn after the departure of Jean-Phillipe Bidart. Owner Charlie Baker posted on the pub's website: 'It is with a great deal of excitement, enthusiasm and personal appreciation I can announce that we are having a true great of the culinary landscape take over the running of the Millbrook kitchen until we locate a permanent head chef to see us back on track for the next part in our journey. I sincerely appreciate John's help taking the reins in the kitchen during this difficult period. Let's hope he enjoys the Millbrook as much as we do and stays long term!' John was happy to help out a friend, but his search continued for a permanent role as an executive chef with leading hotels and restaurants around the world. There were cookery demonstrations to attend and foreign consultancies to enjoy. So maybe he is right when he says he will never stop doing what he loves, and probably will die under a hot oven in some hot kitchen, in chef's whites soaked in sweat and wrists blistered with heat rashes, surrounded by appetisers and entrées and giant soufflés stacked high on serving trays, the kitchen staff too busy to notice him on the floor until end of service, having presumed he is still on his hands and knees searching for that missing blue plaster.

Now aged in his early 60s, his passion for cooking is still as fired up as ever, as is his passion for life. Martin Blunos recalls one of John's many cars was a sky-blue Porsche 911 with yellow brake calipers. Martin at the time was driving an Audi A4 Turbo. 'John would tell me to follow him, and he would be gone in a cloud of road dust and gravel. I could not keep up with him. He runs his life like that, one that has seen so many ups and downs, and so many people have talked about him behind his back. Well, they are behind him for a reason. I have seen the other side of him, like the time he put my wife and I in a taxi when we left L'Ortolan. He probably wouldn't even remember that, but for me it was very humbling. It just showed his huge generosity. I would have been happy to get on the train and sleep on the floor and end up in Cardiff when I should have got off at Bristol. That was the measure of the guy who could be a real dick, yet he can be equally caring and compassionate. But then, even when he smiles you wonder to yourself whether he is taking the piss! I am sure that talking about his childhood and his culinary journey must be almost like therapy for him, and no doubt he might be thinking, "Someone else can have all my crap and maybe they can see why I am like I am".'

The principle of great cooking is knowledge, so when I talk to John, I comprehend the understanding of the process, the ingredients and the cooking, as well as the dishes themselves. Creativity is built on layer upon layer of knowledge that must be easy to take for granted because it is there instinctively. Many aspiring chefs want to dress the cake without understanding how to make it. Through months of research and interviews, I grew to understand that cooking is about both knowledge and education. If one does not understand the culture or the seasonality or the complexity of a particular ingredient, it is hard to be creative—because creativity is about the ability to understand. That is why some of the simplest dishes can prove to be the most difficult to get right. The artistry and knowledge of the chef is to be able to turn something basic into a fantastic dish. Over those months, I grew to appreciate that chefs never stop thinking about food. Stimulation and focus transcend fatigue. For a chef to create atmosphere alongside a wonderful product, working with the front-of-house team must be as equally important as the food being cooked, the concept of the menu and the ingredients behind it. That creativity is motivated by the desire to continue giving customers a great experience. The challenge for the chef is to ensure that when a diner returns, there is something different for them to come back to. That is where seasonal produce comes into play, as it helps make the evolvement of dishes interesting and varied throughout the year. People need to be excited and inspired, and what is needed is theatre, and John has always had that down to a fine art. While chefs manifest their creations in different ways, the kitchen is the first place of that creative process.

It is easy to suggest that dining has changed in the last 20 years, when in reality what has changed most of all is the atmosphere. Restaurants have become less formal, and the food, like fashion, has moved on. While there is an element of fashion within the food industry, a great dish will always be a great dish, although some part of that dish will always evolve while other dishes may have been inspired by meals that chef has enjoyed at other establishments. The creative chef is also the chef who does not want to become bored, which is why with chefs such as John Burton-Race, even the old classic dishes he had become famous for and helped cement his reputation have continued to evolve. They may have changed in appearance, but a great dish will always be a great combination of flavours—made more fitting to suit both the style of cooking and the restaurant in which it is served.

43

HOME TRUTHS

SOMEWHAT AKIN to his life, the current home of John Burton-Race is chaotic. He tells me he likes old stuff, which is probably a good thing, because there is not much new to speak of. 'I live with horses, chickens and dogs, and the house is falling down, and we do not have a single thing that is new. We buy everything from auctions. I like the size of glass where a bottle of red wine goes into two glasses. The cutlery does not match, but it is all silver, and neither do we possess a set of matching plates. I like old stuff.'

He is clearly happy at home, where Suzi is a proper home cook and perfectly happy in all sorts of conditions and all sorts of environments—but she cannot work in a kitchen with her husband because he simply takes over. 'When we lived in the cottage in Strete we cooked on a solid fuel Rayburn from 1945, and when we left the cottage the new people replaced it with a log burner,' she tells me. 'We had so many brilliant meals on that Rayburn. We would fill it up with anthracite and cook everything on it. I had this huge casserole dish and I remember this one particular dinner party for 15 people when I cooked three huge chickens standing up in the oven, because it was so small. All three birds had a different stuffing. As there was no heat regulation. If we wanted to cool the oven down, we would simply open the door or close up all the vents to keep food warm.'

I like Suzi. She is intelligent, down-to-earth, extremely funny and fun to be with; a mucker and someone who does not suffer fools gladly. She calls a spade a spade. She is a perfect foil for John. She is also as passionate about food and wine as her husband. When she thinks he is waffling during our conversations, she tells him to concentrate on the matter in hand. But I found that I got more out of John and his scattergun approach. 'I don't mind him doing a 70-hour week because I have to take care of my horses,' Suzi continues. 'I am an only child and love being on my own. I am normally in bed watching a history programme by the time John returns home from work. It has always been the same.' Even today, John tends to sleep for no more than four or five hours a night. He will sit and have a coffee and moan about everybody ... probably to himself. He says he has offended at least a thousand people, possibly millions. It is clear that he does not really care.

Suzi hails from Northamptonshire, and she tells me she 'sort of had two mothers. My real mother was good baker and would make beautiful cakes. She would make this 'ard 'at, which basically is shortcrust pastry flopped over the side of a tin. You put a filet of beef in the middle and peeled potatoes round the outside along with whole onions, pour gravy on it and stick it in the oven. You do not put the beef on the pastry or cover it up, as instead you cut a circle out. It is delicious. My other mother, Tricia, a close family friend, was a really good cook. I lived with her in London from the age of 17. She was like a stepmother to me. We lived in Pembridge Villas off Westbourne Grove in Notting Hill Gate. She would hold huge dinner parties and make wonderful pheasant casseroles and puddings accompanied by lovely wine. She was a bit like John, in that she would never want any help and just wanted to be left to get on with whatever she was cooking. Westbourne Grove had the most amazing Indian, Arabic and Persian restaurants. I remember The Fortune Cookie in Queensway was a brilliant Chinese. We even used to go to a Sudanese restaurant. In Northamptonshire as a girl, at the end of every month my grandmother, mother, father and I would go to eat at the Talbot Hotel in Oundle. I remember the oak staircase was from Fotheringay Castle, which is where Mary, Queen of Scots was beheaded.' No doubt John would be the first to admit that his wife has a better mental capacity for recollecting times, events and impressions than himself.

EPILOGUE

JOHN BURTON-RACE'S destiny has only ever lain in his own hands. From the challenges and complexities associated with a dysfunctional childhood, which at times saw him become an emotional wreck, he grew an inner strength through resilience and self-determination; emotions that would prove pivotal to his development. And while temperance and wisdom and piety were never virtues that would come easily to him, he would learn to find sanctuary in the kitchen, a place which would forever bring him freedom of expression. It was where he could play by his own rules as he continued to re-define the art of culinary creativity. While he knew he could not buy knowledge, he quickly learnt that he could harvest it to his advantage. Even in the cash-strapped world of John Burton-Race, there has always been an element of swashbuckling romanticism in his quest to create something that is not already there. With such a richness of knowledge, born of the realisation that food does not have to be defined by the country from which it originates, he continues to experiment and excel, forever forging new boundaries.

There has been much ink spilt over many an incendiary moment in his career and personal life, and while he continues to skirt the shadowlands of celebrity status, his name bobbing in and out of people's consciousness like a subliminal drip feed, his journey continues to be both a story and an education. Yes, John Burton-Race can be frustrating and contradictory and infuriating and outspoken and complex and, well, downright bloody rude, but on the other hand it is easy to be judgemental when you are dealing partly with character and partly with sincerity. Then throw into the mix the way he's had to manage the cards he was dealt and the world that confronted him. His has never been an easy ride, and without question he has worked monumentally hard to achieve and maintain a level of creative genius unparalleled in his time. Having said that, he will never reach perfection because he knows that there will always be the next stage in the process — the next culinary hurdle to clear, the hamster treading the circle of infinity.

At our very first meeting, John told me he wanted the biography to show him in a positive light, because at the time he was not feeling terribly positive about himself. 'I would like it to be fun, otherwise why would you read it? I don't want some people to put the book down having said it's an amazing read, only then to find loads of other people feeling suicidal and jumping off bridges into rivers because, quite frankly, I have got enough responsibility already and I can't be doing with any more.' Perhaps that upturned lifeboat may come in useful after all ... once John Burton-Race has managed to turn it the right way up. Just don't hold your breath.

ACKNOWLEDGEMENTS

EVERYONE IN the culinary world would appear to have a story to tell about John Burton-Race. That in itself should come as no surprise when you consider how many household names he has worked with over such a long and distinguished career. For my part, delving into John's life brought both challenges and rewards, and afforded me the opportunity to meet some truly inspirational people. John was only too willing to open up about his childhood and career, even though his scattergun recollections often proved difficult to piece together. Dates seemed to elude him easily, and often I found myself tripping over cuttings or contacting family members to get to the truth, which is why I remain eternally grateful to his delightful sisters, Clare Holmes (née Burton) and Rebecca Race, for inviting me into their homes to talk so candidly about their brother. Thank you both, and especially John, for trusting me to tell your story and for allowing others to help fill in the blanks.

Despite my formal requests, telephone conversations and follow-up emails confirming times, dates and places, Amelia and Charles, John's two children from his second marriage to Kim, eventually decided not to meet with me, and any further communication from my end was to fall on deaf ears. While this was disappointing not only for myself but also for John, in a way I could understand it, as John's marriage had ended in much acrimony and he had little contact with his children over the intervening years, though it was pleasing to learn that the children's relationship with their father eventually turned a corner. John was also happy to point out that no matter the bitterness felt within the family, he could not fault the way in which Kim had brought their children up, and he remains extremely proud of them.

I am extremely grateful to John's daughter Naomi, who was happy to speak with me. The pair share a very good relationship and see each other once or twice a year, interspersed with phone calls and WhatsApp messages.

And I am pleased to say that John's third wife, Suzi, was only too happy to invite me into their home. It was to prove the first occasion that she had actually spoken openly about their relationship, and I remain grateful to her for her openness and honesty. Their son, Pip, who turned 15 years old in December 2019, is, I must confess, a chip off the old kitchen chopping block. Very much an outdoorsy person, he loves horse riding with his mum and is also a keen rugby player. As for food, he enjoys every given opportunity to dine with his parents, particularly when they holiday in France, and is fast becoming a fine purveyor of wines, having already amassed a sound knowledge which belies his youth. Pip has yet to decide on his chosen career but is happy to comment that should he follow in his father's footsteps he would make a far better chef. Anyway, he says candidly, his father probably won't be around for much longer…

Many of the chefs I contacted were happy to spend time away from their busy kitchens to reminisce, standing by John during troubled times and applauding him for his extraordinary successes. That is a measure of true friendship. Knowing their hectic schedules, I was pleasantly surprised that they afforded me so much of their valuable time. At Le Gavroche, Michel Roux Junior was saying his goodbyes to a television crew as I entered the restaurant. Michael Caines was between meetings with his staff. Seated in Raymond Blanc's office at Le Manoir, I was fascinated as chefs came and went throughout the afternoon bearing experimental dishes for him to taste, suggesting soupçons of refinement, passing a chocolate dessert across the table to me and asking my opinion of something that, to my taste buds, was already perfect. Therefore, I am eternally grateful to Raymond Blanc, Gary Jones, Michael Caines, Michel Roux Senior, Michel Roux Junior, Martin Blunos and Stephen Humphreys for being so honest and open with me. The geography of this biography followed a linear path, and with every stone unturned there appeared to be a new demon or ghost to contend with, but without the chefs' input, this book would only be half the story. If they provoked a thought or made you laugh in these pages, then all is well with the world.

I would like to thank my immediate family for their amazing encouragement, support and belief in me, words soporific in their predictability but heartfelt all the same. My mother Wynne, wife Diane, sister Michelle and brother-in-law Graham have grown accustomed to the fact that so long as I have a pen to hand, my desire to write will never wain and my curiosity will never be quenched.

My journey with John began in July 2018 and involved a great deal of travel, interviews, research and lonely night-time vigils in front of the computer screen. Writing a biography is never easy. Finding the right publisher willing to take on a manuscript can prove even harder. Special thanks go to Steven O'Hara, publisher at Mortons Books, for being brave enough to take it on; my editor, Lucy Wood, for being so incredibly thorough and understanding during the many revisions, her pedantry was appreciated; cover designer Rosie Ward for her patience in the various image changes; and Kelvin Clements for his mastery at layout.

Finally, to all the weirdos, curios, wannabees, motivators and encouragers who inhabit kitchens the world over, may your creations remain forever thought-provoking.

Michael Cowton

ABOUT THE AUTHOR

Journalist, author and biographer Michael Cowton has worked variously in the UK, South Africa and Kenya. A former national newspaper journalist, magazine editor and visiting lecturer in media studies, his previous books include Level 42 – The Definitive Biography, Pet Shop Boys – Introspective, and Murders That Shocked The World—1970s, the first in a trilogy of murder titles for Mortons Books. He once attended the rather posh Alain Ducasse Cooking School on rue du Ranelagh in the heart of Paris's 16th arrondissement, where he was shown how to prepare John Dory and artichoke three ways. He still has the apron to prove it.

Michael Cowton